MY BELOVED IS MINE

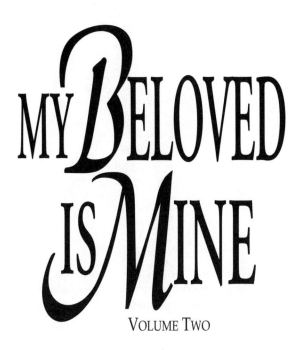

MY BELOVED IS MINE

VOLUME TWO

JOHN W. BRAMHALL

GOSPEL FOLIO PRESS
P. O. Box 2041, Grand Rapids MI 49501-2041
Available in the UK from
JOHN RITCHIE LTD., Kilmarnock, Scotland

Originally published as regular correspondence to interested friends. Some letters have been previously published in *Counsel* magazine, *Uplook* magazine, and elsewhere.

Cover design by J. B. Nicholson, Jr.

Cover photo by Dan Spoelstra,
Spoelstra Studios, Grand Rapids, Michigan

Published by Gospel Folio Press
P. O. Box 2041, Grand Rapids MI 49501-2041

ISBN 1-882701-10-0

Printed in the United States of America

.

"My beloved is white and ruddy,
the chiefest among ten thousand...
His mouth is most sweet:
yea, he is altogether lovely.
This is my beloved, and this is my friend."

(Song of Solomon 5:10, 16)

Contents

Foreword

It was one of those days that autumn had borrowed from summer. Harvest was well under way in the sun-drenched fields south of Augusta, Georgia. John Bramhall was the seasoned veteran; I was the greenhorn preacher. We were both having ministry meetings in the area, and I had asked if I might spend a few hours with him that afternoon. He had graciously consented.

Somewhere along the way, I asked him the question: "Brother Bramhall, of all the needs among the Lord's people today, what do you think is the greatest?" If I had known the man and his ministry better then, I could have anticipated his answer.

"J. B., what we need today is what we have always needed—more devotion to Christ."

Twenty years have passed since that golden afternoon. Since then, I have had the privilege of sharing conference ministry with Mr. Bramhall and collaborating with him on the *Choice Gleanings Calendar,* for which he has been a faithful contributor. (He would often sign his letters to me, "The other J. B.") Yet it does not seem to matter where he begins; it is not long until John Bramhall finds his way to Christ.

But is it not *practical* ministry we need? The apostle Paul would insist that this *is* the most intensely practical ministry available: "But we all, with open face beholding as in a [mirror] the glory of the Lord, are changed into the same image from glory to glory even as by the Spirit of the Lord" (2 Cor. 3:18).

You will not travel far through these chapters without the blessed companionship of Heaven's lovely Man. You will feel yourself as others have felt under the ministry of the author: that you are on the Emmaus Road as evening falls. The sun is melting its gold upon the walls and houses of Jerusalem behind you and the verdant Beth-horon Pass lies at your feet. But you hardly notice. Your heart burns within you as you listen to the words of this Stranger, His lips like lilies dropping sweet-smelling myrrh. You have lost sight of the writer; your heart has been captured by the Son of God. You will lay down the book reluctantly. It is my prayer that, like the two on the road that evening, you will constrain Him to abide with you. He will be happy to oblige.

J. B. Nicholson, Jr.
Grand Rapids, Michigan

Part One
The Grandeur of God

J.R. Bramhall

1
God & Me

"When I consider Thy heavens, the work of Thy fingers, the moon and the stars, which Thou hast ordained; what is man, that Thou art mindful of him? and the son of man, that Thou visitest [regardest] him?"
(Psalm 8:3-4)

When considering the greatness and the glory of the visible universe, David was filled with wonder and amazement that an infinite Creator should manifest any interest in sinful man. The immensity of God's creation exposes the insignificance of humanity. Through the aid of the telescope, astronomers have pushed back the frontiers of the universe known to us by a distance equal to that which light can span in billions of years. "Our present horizon," one has said, "is six trillion billion miles away; and beyond that horizon, we are informed there are thresholds yet to be crossed." Surely we say with David, "The heavens declare the glory of God, and the firmament showeth His handiwork" (Ps. 19:1).

Yet man's insignificance is further revealed through the following: if a man's body were separated into each chemical element, and if we could cause the atoms to collapse, leaving only the matter, the body would suddenly become the merest fleck of dust, visible only under a high-powered microscope.

"What is man, that thou art mindful of him?" Such immensity, staggering our own minds, raises the question: Why should this infinite Creator have the slightest regard for sinful men? Yet this is true: God does regard every individual He has created.

The preaching of the gospel presents this great fact: that God, the Creator of heaven and earth, has a personal concern for each of us. You can say with me: "God is definitely interested in me!" A few well chosen scriptures will verify this statement. Let us, by the Holy Spirit, learn some truths concerning the great God and me.

1. *I am the object of divine creation:* In Psalm 119:73, we hear the Psalmist say to God, "Thy hands have made me and fashioned me." In beautiful simplicity and sublime faith, he acknowledges that I am the object of divine creation. All speculative theories of man's origins are discarded as we confess ourselves to be the work of God's hands. God said, "Let Us make man in Our image, after Our likeness" (Gen. 1:26), and the creative record declares, "The Lord God formed man of the dust of the ground, and breathed into his nostrils the breath of life; and man became a living soul" (Gen. 2:7). Thus was completed the desire of an infinite Creator to have for Himself a creature such as man, for divine fellowship and for His glory. On the authority of God's Word, I say with David, "Thy hands have made me and fashioned me." God made me! Spirit, soul and body, I came from Him.

2. *I am the object of divine contemplation:* In Genesis 16, we have the story of a servant girl named Hagar, bond-slave to Abraham's wife, Sarah, who, being driven by hatred and jealousy from Abraham's home, finds that the Angel of the Lord is overshadowing her in the place of danger and possible death. She is encouraged to return to her mistress and is promised protection as well as divine blessing. Upon this discovery that a heavenly God is interested in a poor Egyptian bond-slave, she addresses Him with these words of appreciation, "Thou God seest me" (Gen. 16:13). Surely this is a confession all should make; every person should acknowledge with Hagar this wonderful fact: I am the object of divine contemplation.

I frankly admit that the God who created me has never failed to observe my life, from the moment of my entrance into His universe to this present time. God Himself declares, "Neither is there any creature that is not manifest in His sight; but all things are naked and opened unto the eyes of Him with whom we

14

have to do" (Heb. 4:13). Your life and mine have never been out of the range of divine contemplation. "Thou God seest me," is a solemn and searching truth.

To all who are the children of God, it is a comforting truth that we have a God who constantly watches over His own. When we find ourselves in difficulties, the fact of a heavenly Father's care lifts us above the circumstances to rejoice in the Lord. To one who is unsaved and far from God, traveling the broad road to destruction, it is soul-convicting to realize that an Omnipotent eye is observing my sinful heart and path. It is useless to hide; any attempt to get away from the eyes of God is as vain as that made by our first parents in the Garden of Eden. God sought them, saying, "Adam, where art thou?" Let every sinner heed the warning of the Lord Jesus, "Nothing is secret, that shall not be made manifest" (Lk. 8:17).

3. *I am the object of divine consideration:* In Psalm 40:17, we read, "But I am poor and needy; yet the Lord thinketh upon me." God made me with His hands, sees me with His eye, and the Scripture reveals He thinks of me with His mind. What condescension! In my poverty, the poverty of my guilty soul, yet He thinks of me. How much have I forgotten Him? Days and hours of careless living have been mine, proving His own words, "There is none that seeketh after God. They are all gone out of the way: they are together become unprofitable; there is none that doeth good, no, not one" (Rom. 3:11-12). But, amazing thought, God has not forgotten me. "The Lord thinketh upon me."

The Psalmist declares in Psalm 139:17-18 the greatness of the divine thoughts to unworthy man: "How precious also are Thy thoughts unto me, O God! How great is the sum of them. If I should count them, they are more in number than the sand." Who can number them? None! Sinner that I am, I am not forgotten by God. He has written, "For I know the thoughts that I think toward you, saith the Lord, thoughts of peace, and not of evil, to give you in your latter end a hope" (Jer. 29:11, JND Trans.) God declares in His Word, to Him I am precious. He values my life (Ps. 72:14); my soul (Ps. 49:6-8); my fellowship (Ps. 133); my service (Ps. 126:6). He even values my death (Ps.

116:15)! Can we begin to exhaust the boundless thoughts of love and grace flowing from the mind of God to His creatures?

4. *I am the object of divine affection:* Inserted in Galatians 2:20 are the following words: "The Son of God, who loved me..." God, we have seen, reveals His hands by creating me; His eye in seeing me; His mind in thinking of me; but here is a greater fact in respect to God and me: He reveals His heart in loving me. I am the object of divine affection. What a tremendous revelation is this—the great God of the universe loves me!

"God commendeth His love toward us, in that while we were yet sinners, Christ died for us" (Rom. 5:8). The apostle John has written, "Herein is love, not that we loved God, but that He loved us and sent His Son to be the propitiation for our sins" (1 Jn. 4:10). Greater are the words of God's own Son to Nicodemus, saying, "For God so loved the world"—telling the *breadth* of His love; "that He gave His only begotten Son"—telling the *length* of His love; "that whosoever believeth in Him should not perish"—telling the *depth* of His love; "but have everlasting life"— telling the *height* of His love. Boundless, matchless, unfathomable and unsurpassable, is the love of God! Will you not say, "I am the object of divine affection"?

5. *I am the object of divine redemption:* The concluding words of Galatians 2:20 declare, He "gave Himself for me." Have you noted the progressive revelation of God to us? His hands made me; His eye sees me; His mind thinks of me; His heart loves me. But for my sinful soul to be redeemed, He must come Himself to die for me. The great Creator comes to earth to save me.

Have you looked at the Cross of Calvary, where Christ the mighty God and Creator died for your sin? Surely you will exclaim in worship, wonder, and praise: "The Son of God, who loved me; and gave Himself for me!" God Himself, in the person of His Son, came down from heights of eternal glory to descend to depths of sin and shame, that He might redeem me. We confess we are the object of divine redemption.

The late King Albert of Belgium was once traveling by auto through the battlefields of Europe during the First World War and noticed a wounded Belgian soldier lying in a field. Stopping his car, the good king went to the wounded man to take him where medical aid could be ministered. As he stopped and lifted him in his arms, the soldier opened his eyes and looked into the king's face. Recognizing his deliverer as his own king, he was heard to exclaim, "O, my king! My king has come to save me!" Have you exclaimed, "My King—and my God—has come to save me!"

> *"Down from His glory, ever living story,*
> *My God and Saviour came, and Jesus was His Name,*
> *Born in a manger, to His own a stranger,*
> *A Man of sorrows, tears, and agony.*
>
> *O how I love Him; how I adore Him,*
> *My breath, my sunshine, my all in all.*
> *The great Creator became my Saviour,*
> *And all God's fullness dwelleth in Him."* (W. E. Clibborn)

Surely we bow at His feet, worshiping the great Creator—not alone for His great work of creation, but for that greater work, the immensity of His great redemption.

6. *I am the object of divine habitation:* Paul wrote, "Christ liveth in me" (Gal. 2:20). When by faith Christ becomes mine, my heart becomes the habitation of the Lord. "If any man hear My voice, and open the door, I will come in to him" (Rev. 3:20), is the promise of the Saviour. "That Christ may dwell in your hearts by faith" (Eph. 3:17), was the prayer of Paul. Oh, the glory of this mystery: "Christ in you, the hope of glory" (Col. 1:27).

Many years ago, at the request of a fellow Christian, I called on an old man who was seriously ill. As I knocked at the door, a girl answered, and I asked, "Is Uncle Jim in?" Upon entering, I saw the old fellow seated in front of the fire, wrapped in a blanket and his overcoat. On his lap he held a tray of fried chicken and rice. Taking the situation in at a glance, I said, "Uncle Jim, I'm sorry I came just as you are about to eat your dinner, but if you don't mind, I would like to talk with you while you eat."

"All right," he replied.

"Uncle Jim," I began, "I understand you know a very good Friend of mine."

"Who's that?" he questioned.

"The Lord Jesus," I replied.

"The Lord! The Lord!" shouted the old fellow. Then to the girl, he said, "Here, take my plate. I'm through, I'm through." Not another taste of food would he take. Turning to me again, he shouted, "He's so great! He's so high! He's up there!" and then smiting his breast, he added, "But He's down here, down here with me. With Jim! Yes, the old brother knew he was the object of divine habitation!

What condescending grace that "Christ liveth in me." We rightfully sing, "Oh, what a salvation this, that Christ liveth in me."

6. *I am the object of divine direction:* "He leadeth me" (Ps. 23:2-3), is the testimony of David and of all who now have Christ within; "He leadeth me in paths of righteousness for His name's sake!" Blessed path of divine guidance by His Spirit and His Word. How does He lead, you ask? "For as many as are led by the Spirit of God, they are the sons of God" (Rom. 8:14). Blessed Holy Comforter: "He dwelleth with you and shall be in you" (Jn. 14:17). The Spirit guides through the Word, for "He will guide you into all truth" (Jn. 16:13). So "when thou goest, it (the Word of God) shall lead thee; when thou sleepest, it shall keep thee; and when thou awakest, it shall talk with thee" (Prov. 6:22). Thus, by the indwelling Spirit and the Word of God, the Good Shepherd continues to lead His sheep through this wilderness experience until at last, though led by paths that often are rough and steep, winding and mysterious, yet He "shall bring them to the desired haven." As I think of the final destination of His guidance, I can say with David, "I will dwell in the house of the Lord forever" (Ps. 23:6).

> *"All the way my Saviour leads me;*
> *What have I to ask beside?*
> *Can I doubt His tender mercy,*
> *Who through life has been my Guide?*
> *Heavenly peace, divinest comfort,*
> *Here by faith in Him to dwell:*
> *For I know what e're befall me,*
> *Jesus doeth all things well."* (Fanny J. Crosby)

7. I am the object of divine protection: "Yea, though I walk through the valley of the shadow of death, I will fear no evil; for Thou art with me" (Ps. 23:4-5). This world, with the shadow of death constantly over it, is to the Christian a "great and terrible wilderness, wherein were fiery serpents, and scorpions, and drought, where there was no water" (Deut. 8:15). Nevertheless, "He hath said, I will never leave thee, nor forsake thee. So that we may boldly say, The Lord is my helper, and I will not fear what man shall do unto me" (Heb. 13:5-6).

Fear is an experience that even the godliest have known, for God has approximately 796 references to it in the Scriptures. Yet for the godly He has an antidote for fear: His own protection—"the shadow of the Almighty"—so that we may say, "Thou art with me." A rabbinical leader has pointed out that Psalm 91, which is the Psalm for the protection of the godly, covers fear around the clock. Notice the words of verses 5 and 6:

1. "Thou shalt not be afraid for the terror *by night.*" Not merely literal darkness is implied, but moral and spiritual darkness, which are far greater. Many dark experiences come in the Christian's path. Then we sing, "...the darkness deepens, Lord with me abide." It is deepening rapidly in the world today; the night will soon hold the terror of God's judgment for this Christ-rejecting scene. Let us not become fainthearted and fail to see "the bright and morning star," our blessed Hope. We find some Christians becoming so pessimistic as to be blowing out their candles to see how dark it is! We have a Refuge—we must "abide under the shadow of the Almighty." Thus we will not fear "the terror by night."

2. "Nor for the arrow that flieth *by day.*" David once prayed, "Hide me from the secret counsel of the wicked; from the insurrection of the workers of iniquity; who whet their tongue like a sword, and bend their bows to shoot their arrows, even bitter words; that they may shoot in secret at the perfect" (Ps. 64:2-4). The righteous have always been the object of these attacks—arrows from the hatred of man or Satan. But, "He is my refuge and my fortress: my God; in Him will I trust" (Ps. 91:2).

3. "Nor for the pestilence that walketh *in darkness.*" The word "pestilence" suggests a destroying plague. How many

"plagues" are waiting in the world of "Vanity Fair" to snare and destroy a Christian's testimony. "All that is in the world (1 Jn. 2:15-17) is combined to be a precipice for the saints. Many have been on its edge, but have been mercifully delivered by God. Others may have fallen and were only restored by deep sorrow, repentance and tears. Some have fallen completely over to the destruction of the flesh. Yet for this danger, "He is my refuge." I am the object of divine protection.

4. "Nor for the destruction that wasteth *at noonday*." The hour of success—the noonday of life—finds pride waiting to do its destroying work! This danger is present when we are at the pinnacle of even spiritual success. The devil took the Saviour to a pinnacle of the temple (read Lk. 4:9-13), setting this "snare of the fowler" for Him, even partially quoting Psalm 91 for His encouragement, but that blessed One failed not, through the power of the Word of God! Surely He, in His earthly dependence on God, abode "under the shadow of the Almighty." This is the place for you and me, for night and day, every twenty-four hours.

8. *I am the object of divine completion:* "The Lord will perfect [complete] that which concerneth me" (Ps. 138:8). Through the sovereign counsel of God, dust was my beginning but, through His matchless love and grace, glory will be my ending! Truly I will say, 'Thou art the God that doest wonders" (Ps. 77:14). What shall I be at the completion of His purposes? No better words can tell me than the precious record of 1 John 3:2, "Beloved, now are we the sons of God, and it doth not yet appear what we shall be; but we know that, when He shall appear, we shall be like Him, for we shall see Him as He is." Blessed anticipation!

> *"And is it is so, I shall be like Thy Son,*
> *Is this the grace which He for me has won?*
> *Father of glory, thought beyond all thought,*
> *In glory to His own blest likeness brought."* (J. N. Darby)

"For whom He did foreknow, He also did predestinate to be conformed to the image of His Son" (Rom. 8:29). Yes, every believer now rejoices "in hope of the glory of God" (Rom. 5:2). The Father will have a complete family in His eternal and glori-

20

ous presence, "holy and without blame before Him in love" (Eph. 1:4). What a glad moment it will be to the heart of God the Father, when, from the dust of the earth, redeemed and glorified, the Son shall present all of us to the Father in His own likeness, saying, "Behold I and the children which God hath given me" (Heb. 2:13).

> *"Nor I alone, Thy loved ones all, complete,*
> *In glory round Thee there with joy shall meet,*
> *All like Thee, for Thy glory like Thee, Lord,*
> *Object supreme of all, by all adored."* (J. N. Darby)

Blessed completion—the glorification of the saints at the coming of our Lord and Saviour, Jesus Christ! Surely our hearts re-echo the apostle's cry: "Even so, come, Lord Jesus."

> *"That Thou couldst be a God to me,*
> *And be the God Thou art,*
> *Is darkness to my intellect,*
> *But sunshine to my heart."*

2
Divine Silence

There have been noticeable silences during human history when God seemed to withdraw Himself from the affairs of men without any visible intervention. Here are some examples.

1. In Eden, "the voice of the Lord God" was heard as He walked with man, but it ceased to be heard after the Fall. As His voice faded away, there followed a period of silence as the world embarked on its path of departure from God. The silence was broken by the voice of Enoch, declaring, "Behold, the Lord cometh with ten thousands of His saints…" (Jude 14-15).

2. After Enoch, another long silence set in as the wickedness of earth increased, until God spoke by the loud judgment of the Flood. Noah and his family alone were spared and delivered out of that terrible catastrophe (Gen. 6 & 7).

3. Following the Flood the world was given a fresh start, but soon regressed further away from God until heathen idolatry and moral darkness covered the earth while God kept silent. Then the God of glory appeared to Abraham, calling him out of that darkness to the land of Canaan (Gen. 12:1 and Acts 7:2-4). For 1500 years, from Abraham to Malachi, God began speaking to His earthly people, though periods of silence were also experienced during this epoch.

4. After Malachi, another spell of silence lasted for four centuries, but was suddenly broken by the voice of John the Baptist crying, "Repent ye: for the kingdom of heaven is at hand" (Mt. 3:2). Then began a period of divine revelation in fullness as God spoke though the Person of His Son (Heb. 1:1-3), followed by the

ministry of the Holy Spirit through the Apostles. As the last echoes of His voice died away on Patmos, John records the Lord Jesus, saying, "Behold I come quickly, Amen," and John responds at once, "Even so, Come, Lord Jesus."

5. After Revelation, the longest period of silence set in and has continued all through the Christian era. It has been a long mysterious silence, during which many hearts, under the strain, have cried out, "How long, O Lord, how long?" Will the silence be broken? Will God refuse to intervene in the affairs of this evil world? Why is He so long silent? Peter explains the reason for it: The Lord "is longsuffering to usward, not willing that any should perish, but that all should come to repentance" (2 Pet. 3:9). But there is an exact "day and hour" known to the Father (Mt. 24:36) when the long silence will be broken and "Our God shall come, and shall not keep silence" (Ps. 50:3). It will be at "the glorious appearing of the great God and our Saviour Jesus Christ" (Titus 2:13). Then it will be said, "The God of glory thundereth" (read Ps. 29). His powerful voice will be "as the sound of many waters" (Rev. 1:15). All shall hear His voice.

The breaking of God's silence is the particular theme of Psalm 50. The Psalm divides itself into three sections, relating to the saints (v. 5); to Israel (v. 7); and to the wicked (v. 16).

IN RELATION TO THE SAINTS (vv. 1-6)

The majesty of His coming is revealed by the array of His titles: "El Elohim Jehovah" in the Hebrew text. Literally He is called "God, the Mighty God Jehovah hath spoken." The first two imply that He is the mighty God of judgment who will be a terror to the wicked. His name Jehovah reveals His coming as the faithful Covenant-keeper of redemption, to gather His saints together and consummate His eternal purposes for them. As He breaks the silence, the whole universe will hear His voice— "from the rising of the sun until the going down thereof." It is announced as if already done: "Out of Zion...the Lord *hath* shined." It is the Old Testament proclamation of the Epiphany.

As to the manner of His coming (v. 3), "a fire shall devour before Him" when His voice breaks the silence of the centuries. It will astonish the whole world from one end to the other with the blaze of His glory. What inevitable destruction is involved! (Read Isa. 30:30; Isa. 66:15-16; 2 Thess. 1:8-9.)

What is the object of His coming (vv. 4-6)? More important to Him than judgment will be the gathering of His redeemed people together from the heavens and the earth. The saints of all ages will be claimed by Him and for Him. His "shout" will break the silence of the graves and change the living saints, catching them up together to meet Him "in the air" (1 Thess. 4:13-18). He will then turn His attention toward the saints of earth and out of the chaos and strife gather them together. When His purpose toward the saints is accomplished, "the heavens shall declare His righteousness." Hallelujah!

IN RELATION TO ISRAEL (vv. 7-15)

The restoration of Israel is heralded (v. 7). He calls them "My people," showing that the Lo-Ammi period is ended and that Israel has become Ammi (see Hos. 1:9-10). Like doubting Thomas, when the remnant acknowledge Him, they will say, "My Lord and my God" (Jn. 20:28). He will say to them—"I am God, even thy God!"

Then we are reminded of His controversy with Israel (vv. 8-14). In substance, this section presents God's argument about their ritual services and sacrifices. He, as the possessor of all the earth, did not need their flocks; what He was seeking from them was the appreciation of their hearts for Him and the devotion of their lives. This they had failed to give Him. Each sacrifice should have been accompanied by their affection and by the keeping of their solemn vows (v. 14).

In the deliverance of Israel (v. 15), He will call them "My people," after they have passed through the purging fire of the Great Tribulation (Jer. 30:7; Mt. 24:21). In that day they will hear Him say, "Call upon Me in the day of trouble, I will deliver thee, and thou shalt glorify Me." The time is prophesied in Zechariah 13:8-9, when a remnant will be saved not only from outward oppression but free from inward sin and unbelief.

IN RELATION TO THE WICKED (vv. 16-23)

A careful reading indicates that the professors of God's name and Word come under His special judgment as He breaks the silence of earth. Will there not be many "foolish virgins"? (Mt. 25:1-13). Will there not be many "tares"? (Mt. 13:24-30). Will there not be many apostates? (2 Tim. 3:1-5; 2 Pet. 2; Jude 1-17). These have hated God's instructions and cast His words behind them, whether Jews or Gentiles. His long silence they have misunderstood to mean their escape, but when He breaks it, they will be visited by the thunderbolts of His wrath without mercy! (see Ps. 50:22).

It is fatal to leave God out. He is ready to show His salvation now to any who will hear His voice and turn to Him: "Today if ye will hear His voice, harden not your hearts" is the exhortation of God's Word (Heb. 4:7). How wonderful the joy of the believer when God says, "Thou shalt call thy walls salvation and thy gates praise" (Isa. 60:18). His long silence has been profitable for the believer. We "account that the longsuffering of our Lord is salvation" (2 Pet. 3:15). May we praise the Lord that we have heard His voice now! May many more hear while He still speaks in grace.

3
The Home of the Heart

Psalm 84, the Sanctuary Psalm, leads the heart to the heart of God. Note the outline of it in three sections:

1. *The heart's desire—to find God* (vv. 1-4). Notice the heart's attraction: "How amiable (lovely) are Thy tabernacles." The majesty and beauty of the temple is not what captivated the psalmist. It was the amicability, the thoughtful friendliness of the place where God's presence dwelt.

There is intensity of desire, too; with his whole being he longed for God. "My soul...heart...flesh...crieth out for the living God." The united object, the sole focus, was God.

Then follows an illustrative lesson, showing us the way to God. The repentant sinner comes like a worthless sparrow, as a restless swallow. If birds are safe in God's altars, then divine grace will shelter all who seek refuge in Christ. Is it the Brazen Altar? Then there is once-for-all refuge in His sacrificial death (Heb. 9:12). Is it the Golden Altar? Then such are preserved through His unfailing intercession (Heb. 7:25).

Notice the happiness there is in finding God. Praise well suits the overflowing heart to sing eternal praises.

2. *The heart's decision—to follow God* (vv. 5-8). Strength for the path is divine: "whose strength is in Thee." This is an essential fact to realize. (See Rom. 7:18; Eph. 6:10; Phil. 4:13; 2 Tim. 2:1). There is also instruction for the path: "In whose heart are the highways" (JND Trans.). The Word of God must abide in the heart. (See Ps. 25:9; Ps. 27:11; Ps. 119:11, 105.)

As well, there is progression in the path. The discipline of tri-

27

als and sorrows come to us "who [are] passing thru the valley of Baca [weeping]." But such sorrows can be changed into blessings. Faith will find a source of refreshment in the darkest valley. The valley experiences are filled with the grace of God, for "the rain filleth the pools" (see 2 Cor. 12:9).

Step by step, the pilgrim presses on; strength increases. "They go from strength to strength." God preserves all who trust Him from fainting and falling. He watches over us: we appear before Him. And He supplies fresh strength abundantly. But dependence on God should be constant: "Hear my prayer," cries out the one in need. We are heartened to come to Him: He is the "Lord God of hosts"—symbolic of His power; He is "the God of Jacob"—symbolic of His grace.

3. *The heart's delight—fellowship with God* (vv. 9-12). The goal is reached—enjoying the sunshine of His love! God looks on the face of His anointed and the heart finds perfect acceptance (Eph. 1:6). Abiding in the Sonshine of Christ's love, fellowship is enjoyed. (See Jn. 14:21, 23; 1 Jn. 1:3.) Did not Jesus say, "The Father Himself loveth you" (Jn. 16:27)? *Here is the home of the heart!* "God is love; and he that dwelleth in love, dwelleth in God and God in him" (l Jn. 4:16).

The humblest service for God is the joy of the heart. Satisfied to know heart fellowship with God and enjoy the secret of His presence, one day there is worth more than thousands elsewhere. We are content to abide in Him, to be near Him, to be in "the house of my God."

Notice God's increasing preciousness—a "sun and shield." He is light and protection all through life. "The Lord will give grace and glory." There is grace for each step of the journey, and at the end there is glory. Oh, the happiness of the heart at home with God. "Blessed [happy] is the man that trusteth in Thee." There is security, strength and serenity when God is the home of the heart.

God longs to be longed for. He loves to be sought,
For He sought us Himself with such longing and love;
He died for desire of us, marvelous thought!
And He yearns for us now to be with Him above.   (F. W. Faber)

28

4
The Knowledge of the Lord

"Then shall we know, if we follow on to know the Lord"
(Hosea 6:3)

There are two classes of Christians. There are wholehearted Christians, so absorbed in Christianity that God is the greatest fact in life; Christ is the greatest joy in life; and the Scriptures, the greatest source of truth for life. But there are also halfhearted Christians, with lukewarm faith and devotion, traveling in the correct outward groove of Christian formalism, having been born again, but devoid of the warmth, power, and liberty of the Spirit of God. And why? Because they fail "to follow on to know the Lord."

In relation to our subject, one has written, "To know this mighty Being as far as He may be known, is the noblest aim of human understanding; to love Him, the most worthy exercise of our affections; to serve Him, the most honorable and delightful purpose to which we can devote our time and talents" (John Dick). But how do we go on in this exploration?

TWO SOURCES OF DIVINE REVELATION

1. *The Book of Nature* (Ps. 19:1-6; Rom. 1:19-20). This source is sufficient evidence of God's "eternal power and Godhead" for all, so man is without excuse if he does not know God. Even so, this line of evidence is not a complete and perfect revelation of God.

2. *The Book of Holy Scripture* (Ps. 19:7-11; 2 Tim. 3:14-17; 2 Cor.

3:18; Heb. 1:1-2). The great theme of Holy Scripture is Christ! The revelation of God's glory is in the face of Jesus Christ "because it is the God who spoke that out of darkness light should come, who has shone in our hearts for the shining forth of the knowledge of the glory of God in the face of Jesus Christ" (2 Cor. 4:6, JND Trans.). This is a complete and perfect revelation of God.

TWO WAYS OF KNOWING GOD

There are two ways of knowing God, as indicated by two Greek words, *oida* and *ginosko*.

1. OIDA indicates the knowledge of the intellect, producing thoughts. It is an intuitive, or inward, conscious knowledge and conveys the thought of immediate perception. For example, the consciousness of knowing who the person is in 2 Timothy 1:12 is an example of *oida*. Also, it is used of the inward knowledge of the Scriptures as in 2 Timothy 3:14-15.

2. GINOSKO signifies objective knowledge, that which a person learns or acquires, a gradual increasing knowledge. In other words, it is to "follow on to know the Lord."

The first word can be termed head knowledge, being merely intellectual and producing thoughts. The second is personal or heart knowledge, which produces feelings. There can be an intelligent understanding of God that may be cold, though clear, as ice, for it is barren and unfruitful apart from heart knowledge of God. Intelligence alone will not produce feelings until the truth affects the heart, but as personal knowledge of God is enjoyed, it leads to a fuller intelligence or understanding of God. So let us realize our God desires His truth to be known, not only in the intellect, but felt in the heart.

HOW TO SEEK THE KNOWLEDGE OF GOD

1. *With a divinely imparted desire.* Our Father even offers to impart the needed wholehearted desire to know Him. "And I will give them a heart to know Me...for they shall return unto Me with their whole heart" (Jer. 24:7). This is a future promise for Israel, yet how much more should we, as His children today, acknowledge His willingness to do this?

2. *With intense earnestness.* (Read Prov. 2:1-5). Emphasize the words: "*Receive* My word...*lay up* My commandments ...*incline* thine ear...*apply* thine heart...*cry after* knowledge...*lift up* thy voice...*seek* for her as silver...*search* as for hid treasures." This speaks of faithful diligence being required in seeking the Lord. But note the result: "Then shalt thou understand and find the knowledge of God." In all this we realize it is impossible for us to comprehend the fullness of God, though He fully comprehends us (see Ps. 139:1-4); yet we may apprehend more of Him and His glory if we will give ourselves diligently to this pursuit of God.

PRACTICAL AND SCRIPTURAL METHODS TO USE

1. *By faith we apprehend God.* This is a vital principle to follow, for "without faith it is impossible to please Him" (Heb. 11:6). The great record of faith's heroes in Hebrews 11 declares that they all knew God and proved Him by faith. What is faith? It is the firm, irrevocable, unquestioning grasp of divinely revealed facts that God unfolds to us by His words and thoughts in Holy Scripture. Faith cannot and will not doubt, but will accept with confidence the teaching of His Book.

2. *By meditation we apprehend God.* In Scripture the word means "waiting on God." Webster defines it as the "solemn reflection on sacred matters, as a devotional act." It is not a passive attitude, but an active reaching out by my spirit toward God. With faith, meditation is not just mental assent but the mental assimilation or eating of the facts revealed by God in His Word. (Read Jer. 15:16; Ps.104:34; 1 Tim. 4:14.) Mental assimilation of God's Word will form an actual part of our character.

> "*Only to sit and think of God,*
> *Oh! what a joy it is!*
> *To think the thought, to breathe the name,*
> *Earth has no higher bliss.*"

3. *By prayer we apprehend God.* This is not merely *asking of God,* but rather the all-inclusive meaning of prayer: *communion with God.* Personal knowledge of God will transform our prayers from mere asking to the act of pouring our heart to Him in love,

adoration, and praise. So often must we confess that our outward knowledge of God far exceeds our communion with God. Prayer should bring us into the sanctuary of His presence where we worship and adore Him in love and praise.

> *"There's not a craving in the mind*
> *Thou dost not meet and still;*
> *There's not a wish the heart can have*
> *Which Thou dost not fulfill.*
>
> *O little heart of mine! shall pain*
> *Or sorrow make thee moan,*
> *When all this God is all for thee,*
> *A Father all thine own?*
>
> *With gentle swiftness lead me on,*
> *Dear God! to see Thy face.*
> *And meanwhile in my narrow heart*
> *Oh! make Thyself more space."*   (F. W. Faber)

5
How Knowing God Changes Me

Personal knowledge of God will change character, performing transformations which follow the new birth. It is gradual, not sudden change, as the Spirit of God introduces new motives and objects into the life for God's glory (2 Cor. 3:18). "Christianity in its revelation of a personal God and Saviour, of a future life, and of moral responsibility, and its view that the glory of God rather than the mere pleasure of man is the highest object of life, is the most powerful force in the formation of character" (A. T. Schofield, M. D. from *Springs of Character*).

Therefore, we turn from modern philosophy and ethics, preferring "the depths of God" to man's shallow pride, for we must "dwell deep" (Jer. 49:8).

> *Dwell deep, my soul!— forbid thou shouldest stay shallow!*
> *Dwell deep in thought, in purpose, wish and will!*
> *Dwell deep in God—let His own presence hallow;*
> *Thy inner being let His presence fill.*

1. *The mind is changed by a personal knowledge of God.* "The mind casts a shadow just like the body," it has been said. As we pass through this world, unknown to ourselves, our personality, without effort or desire, is casting shadows for good or evil on those whom we meet. To know God is to be a blessing, for then we can be the unconscious channel through which God passes into the hearts of others. Unconsciously we radiate His glories as we live in the personal enjoyment of God.

The sphere of the mind has been called "the hidden home of

character." Therefore we hear the Spirit plead for "the renewing of your mind" in Romans 12:2. It implies "a renovation, a complete change for the better" (*Thayer's Lexicon*). "Being renewed in the spirit of your mind; and having put on the new man" (Eph. 4:23-24) is to be so changed that the spirit which governs the mind is renewed. What a change! The wisdom and knowledge of God is revealed to one who is spiritual: "But we have the mind of Christ" (1 Cor. 2:6-16). "We are said—having the Holy Spirit—to have also the mind of Christ, the intelligent faculty with its thoughts" (footnote in JND Trans.). An appreciation of Romans 11:33-36 will help us fulfill Romans 12:1-2.

2. *The desires are changed by a personal knowledge of God.* "Be ye transformed by the renewing of your mind," writes Paul. The renewing of the mind will produce, without effort on our part, a change of desires. The word "transformed" indicates "a change of moral character for the better, a process of changing" (*Thayer*). How greatly should this be desired! How the habits of life, which we earnestly would have altered, can be changed for us by the Spirit.

It is harmful for us to attempt changing habits without changing desires; no progress is made and nothing is gained. On every hand Christians ask, "Is it right? Is this wrong?" It is unspiritual to do so, for to give up anything without changing desires is only to be a hypocrite. The change of desires is made by the transforming work of the Spirit and involves no giving up. Draw near to God; learn to know Him; the result is—the desires are changed. There is no loss; nothing but gain. (Read Ps. 73:25-26; 37:4.) The old desires (Eph. 2:3) disappear; the new desires conform to the will of God.

3. *The manners are changed by a personal knowledge of God.* It is an evidence of God's power when our manners are changed, for they will be compatible to God's character and reveal us to be a friend of God. Abraham "was called the friend of God" (see 2 Chron. 20:7; Jas. 2:23). What behavior and deportment must have been reflected in Abraham through this intimate friendship with God.

Enoch walked with God three hundred years (Gen. 3:21-24; Heb. 11:5). He had no Bible as we do; no Christianity as we know it; no revealed Father as we have. Yet what a life! God became his nearest and dearest Friend as he walked with Him all those years. What must have been the character of his deportment? What were the results of such a walk? There would be an unassuming and humble dignity in his earthly life. And truth and sincerity in perfect wisdom must have been reflected in perfect love. An inward peace and calm would be seen in his manners, though surrounded by antedeluvian sin and wickedness. How we should seek to possess this unconscious stamp of God upon our manners in these perilous times (see Isa. 26:3).

4. *The pursuits of life are changed by a personal knowledge of God.* This follows the change of desires, for the pursuits of life will be definitely affected by our increasing knowledge of God. The inward change of desires must precede the outward change in pursuits. If not, the outward change will be artificial and also contrary to the principles of Christianity. Christianity is the life of Christ working from within and outward in its direction (Gal. 2:20). It is the life of Christ communicated to the believer, dwelling in the believer and to flow through the believer.

When God works within (Phil. 2:12-13), there will be the necessary change of pursuits, for He Himself will fill the vision. We can be just as keen in our pursuits but after different objects than formerly. Instead of man—God will be in the foreground of life. Man will shrink to his proper perspective, and pursuit of God will change the pursuits of life! Let the wilderness Psalm of David be the earnest cry of our hearts—Psalm 63, noting particularly verses 1, 5 and 8.

5. *The heart is content in a personal knowledge of God.* The world seeks for contentment but apart from God. It drinks from sources that can only fail (see Jer. 2:13; 17:13; Jn. 4:14). How different are the words of Paul, "I have learned in those circumstances in which I am, to be satisfied" (Phil. 4:11, JND Trans.). Christ was his source of satisfaction. Contentment, satisfaction, harmony, holiness, and wholeness of spirit are in Him (see Jn. 4:14; 1 Tim. 6:6). The sight of God changes all—even one's self; and how needful is this. "Now mine eye seeth Thee," said Job, "wherefore I abhor myself and repent in dust and ashes" (Job 42:6). How simple and sweet life is when "my heart is fixed"

35

(see Ps. 57:7; 108:1; 112:7).

6. *The man is conquered by a personal knowledge of God.* There always seems to be a war in our members (Rom. 7; Gal. 5:17), but if we lived in the reality of God's presence there would not be that constant conflict. The reason our evil natures and fleshly desires make such a strong fight within, is simply because we do not know God as we ought.

When God is the Victor, there is no battle; there is no strife. The power and value of heart knowledge of God will show that His love conquers; love that is not constrained, nor forced, but spontaneous love. There can be no fight where God is known: "Not I, but Christ" (Gal. 2:20).

7. *The thoughts are changed by a personal knowledge of God.* The personal knowledge of God will affect each thought I think and each word I speak. He is to be the central truth of my life, the pivot around which my existence revolves. When I know Him as I should—that He is all-wise, all-loving, all-powerful—I will not seek to explain, defend or still less, question His dealings with me. My thoughts of God in my inmost soul will be with deepest reverence and love. My thoughts will be guarded by Him. How greatly we need this!

"The Lord is near; be careful about nothing; but in everything, by prayer and supplication with thanksgiving, let your requests be made known unto God: and the peace of God, which surpasses every understanding, shall guard your hearts and your thoughts by Christ Jesus" (Phil. 4:5-7, JND Trans.). Let us permit God Himself to form our character and personality.

6
The God of Hope

"Now the God of hope fill you with all joy and peace in believing, that ye may abound in hope, through the power of the Holy Ghost"
(Romans 15:13)

When God speaks of Himself as "the God of hope," it proves conclusively that there is no element of uncertainty connected with it. He is not the God of uncertainties.

Hope in the Scriptures is a combination of desire and expectation that is founded on the promises of God. The soul that believes His Word longs to possess His promises and expects them by faith.

Yet faith and hope, though closely linked together, should not be confused with each other. Faith looks backward and hope looks onward; faith is concerned with the Person who promises, but hope is concerned with the promise being fulfilled. Faith accepts while hope expects. Faith appropriates but hope anticipates. Faith believes and takes, while hope desires and waits. Faith comes by hearing but hope by experience. Faith is a root and hope is a fruit.

Consider the hopelessness of the world: "Having *no hope* and without God in this world" (Eph. 2:12). We are living in days when the world is indeed hopeless! In years past, men had the hope that the world was getting better. They taught that man was, by evolutionary process, improving and would rise to a higher plane in which the brotherhood of man would be universal. But by the cataclysm of two world wars during this century that hope has been exploded. In spite of this, the world continues to build other hopes which in turn will also be dashed to pieces. The nations still cry, "Peace, peace, when there is no peace" (Jer. 6:14). They have not profited from past experience and still dare to hope for peace, ignoring what God says in His Word, "There is no peace, saith the Lord, unto the wicked" (Isa. 48:22; 57:21).

Man's hope is a strong delusion from Satan, the god of this world, a vain dream resting on a broken foundation, on man himself, who is a hopeless wreck. Without God, man has no hope!

Consider the hope of Israel. To one nation alone has God provided a definite hope—the seed of Abraham. What is their hope? It is an earthly dominion of worldwide supremacy, an everlasting kingdom (Isa. 60). Their hope is centered in one Person who will come and establish that kingdom, will manifest His supremacy, and take the dominion of the world for Himself (Ps. 2; Ps. 47-48; Ps. 110).

Is this a dream? No! It is the God-given hope of Israel. Paul believed it and suffered for it (Acts 26:6-7; 28:20). There is to be one universal King on the earth (Zech. 14:9); one Righteous ruler (Isa. 32:1); one worldwide Monarch (Rev. 11:15); one King of Glory reigning on Zion's hill (Ps. 2:6; Ps. 24). All nations shall bring homage to Israel's King (Isa. 2:1-5; Zech. 14:16). His presence on earth will secure the restoration and blessing of Israel (Isa. 61).

The animal creation will be delivered from its present brutality; the lion and the lamb will gambol together with a little child able to lead them (Isa. 11:6-9). The curse will be lifted; thistles will oppress no more; even the desert shall bloom as a rose (Rom. 8:19-21).

How well do we grasp this wonderful vision concerning the Hope of Israel and the universal blessing it will bring to the earth? Here is abundant material of divine revelation for us to dream dreams—which are not dreams at all, but a blessed and certain promise of God. If God could open the eyes of a man like Balaam, a false prophet, to see what others could not see, surely we enlightened children of God should behold with our eyes of faith what to others is veiled and lost (read Num. 24). It is no delusive daydream! The God of Hope has set this before His people Israel and one Person is the center of it all—Christ, Israel's coming Messiah.

Consider the hope of the creation. The believer's hope does not rest on man or the earth. We turn our gaze toward heaven, to our glorified Lord who is our Hope (1 Tim. 1:1). "Beloved, now are we the sons of God, and it doth not yet appear what we shall be; but we know that, when He shall appear, we shall be like Him; for we shall see Him as He is" (1 Jn. 3:2). Did not the Saviour promise us: "I will come again, and receive you unto Myself; that where I am, there ye may be also" (Jn. 14:3)? This is our hope! We shall be with Him! We shall be like Him! We shall see Him!

While waiting, however, we can find present power and blessing in our hope.

1. *The hope ministers joy.* We are to "rejoice in hope of the glory of God" (Rom. 5:2). This is the portion of all justified believers. Our final joy is to be "conformed to the image of His Son" (Rom. 8:29), the divine purpose for all God's children. What a sure basis for rejoicing as we journey to our home in glory, our Father's house! The end will be better than the anticipation. So let us be "rejoicing in hope; patient in tribulation" (Rom. 12:12). "The way may be rough, but it cannot be long, so we'll smooth it with hope and cheer it with song."

2. *The hope ministers comfort.* This world of sorrow that we travel through brings us face to face with "the king of terrors" (Job 18:14). But God has given to His people who "believe that Jesus died and rose again" a blessed hope as we stand by our beloved dead. We hear Him say, "Them also that sleep in Jesus will God bring with Him" (l Thess. 4:14). What a happy and eternal reunion will follow (1 Thess. 4:16-17)! Multitudes have received comfort from God through this precious promise. Though we may mourn in this valley of sorrows, strength is ministered to our aching hearts by His exhortation: "Wherefore comfort one another with these words" (4:18). Oh, how many things will the Rapture fix!

3. *The hope ministers endurance.* It is a practical hope of encour-

agement, for while we "wait for His Son from heaven," God exhorts us to be "serving the true and living God" (1 Thess. 1:9-10). After revealing the mystery of resurrection and the transformation of both dead and living, Paul exhorts us to be "steadfast, unmoveable, always abounding in the work of the Lord" (1 Cor. 15:58).

The hope presents our responsibility to endure by His grace, encouraging us when storms of circumstances sweep across the path, for this hope is "an anchor of the soul" (Heb. 6:19), ministering endurance when we are ready to faint.

4. *The hope ministers faithfulness.* Our hope also reminds us that when the Lord comes, our service and stewardship will be appraised by Him at the Judgment Seat of Christ. It will be the accounting day, the review of our personal faithfulness, for "the day shall declare it, because it shall be revealed by fire; and the fire shall try every man's work of what sort it is" (1 Cor. 3:13). Therefore, this blessed hope is to have a refining influence on our present motives and encourage us to be faithful until He comes. It is written: "Moreover it is required in stewards, that a man be found faithful" (1 Cor. 4:2). God grant we shall hear His approval in that day: "Well done, thou good and faithful servant" (Mt. 25:21).

5. *The hope ministers moral conformity to Christ.* The apostle John writes, "Every man that hath this hope in him purifieth himself, even as He is pure" (1 Jn. 3:3). This is the only place he uses the word "hope." The hope produces purity of heart, mind, and life in the believer.

Therefore, if this is our hope, we are to be found now "rejoicing in hope" (Rom. 12:12). We are also to "abound in hope" (Rom. 15:13). We are to "lay hold upon the hope set before us" (Heb. 6:18). Did you ever consider that today may be the last day to hope for all this? He may come today. But if not, we must still "hope to the end." He is coming!

What better benediction can we hear after our meditation than the words written by the beloved Apostle Paul: "Now the God of hope fill you with all joy and peace in believing, that ye may abound in hope, through the power of the Holy Ghost" (Rom. 15:13).

7

His Incomparable Love

*"For God so loved the world that He gave His only begotten Son,
that whosoever believeth in Him should not perish
but have everlasting life"* (John 3:16).

With infinite, incomparable and revealing words, twenty-five in English, the Son of God declares the fullness of God's love toward us. None but "the only begotten Son" who is in the bosom of the Father (Jn. 1:18) could do this. Meditate with me on this inexhaustible theme which we will enjoy for time and eternity:

1. *The unworthy objects of His love:* "For God so loved *the world*" of mankind! Consider seriously the character and conduct of the world to God. Think of its moral condition, it's character in His sight: "dead in sins" (Eph. 2:4-5); consisting of "the ungodly" (Rom. 5:6, 8); they have no love for God (1 Jn. 4:10). Yet, the Highest in the universe stooped the lowest to prove His love for us. His love was not limited by distance, for it "shineth in darkness" (Jn. 1:5, down to the darkness of human sin, His love is not limited by time, for it is an "everlasting love" (Jer. 31:3). Nor is it limited by the awful fact of the world's condition—"guilty before God" (Rom. 3:19). Conclusively we must confess that the whole habitable world is unworthy of God's love.

2. *The magnitude of His sacrifice:* "He gave His only begotten Son." The greatest love must be measured by the immensity of its gift. God, to prove His perfect love, did not give any creature

41

to save us—not an angel, nor a battalion of angels—but "His only begotten Son," heaven's richest treasure and the ineffable delight of His Father heart. "This is My beloved Son, in whom I have found My delight" (Mt. 3:17, JND Trans.). The Son was dearer to the heart of His Father than Isaac was to Abraham. (Compare Gen. 22:2 with Heb. 11:17.)

Two great facts are revealed concerning God's love for us by the gift of His Son. It reveals the sincerity of His love. And it reveals the intensity of His love. How can our minds fathom such depths? Yet we echo Paul's words: "Thanks be unto God for His unspeakable gift." How true that it is "love that no thought can reach; love that no tongue can teach."

3. *The sublime purpose of His love:* "Whosoever believeth in Him should not perish." His grand purpose was the salvation of the world. Such a great God-like love as this, with a great God-like gift, must have a God-like objective. It does! "The man Christ Jesus gave Himself a ransom for all" (1 Tim. 2:6). For God is "not willing that any should perish" (2 Pet. 3:9).

Making the world the object of His love, God sought the highest possible blessing for it. True love will seek the best welfare for its object and God certainly did this. The love of God and the death of Christ are intended to rescue the world of sinners from the greatest calamity—perishing! Instead of hell, God's great love provided the greatest conceivable blessing for man: "everlasting life." What a sublime purpose that could never be greater. Yet, sad is the fact, Satan has blinded the minds of them that believe not. What unbelief prevails.

4. *The simplicity of His method:* It is only by faith, "that whosoever believeth in Him." No other terms, if you please! "For by grace are ye saved through faith; and that not of yourselves: it is the gift of God: not of works, lest any man should boast" (Eph. 2:8-9). The believing sinner can receive complete assurance that God in His love has provided a perfect salvation on the simplest and easiest terms—the exercise of faith! To the penitent, believing sinner the Saviour would say, "Be not afraid, only believe" (Mk. 5:36). When done, He then says to such, "Thy faith hath saved thee; go in peace" (Lk. 7:50). "Beloved, if God *so* loved us, we ought also to love one another" (1 Jn. 4:11).

8
God's Three Great Gifts

The greatest Giver of the universe is God. He freely offers the greatest of His gifts to mankind out of the greatness of His loving heart and through His matchless grace. Any endeavor on our part to present to Him any personal merit for these gifts is colossal folly and only proves we are unworthy to have them. They are free and must be accepted as His gifts of sovereign grace. Though God has given many gifts to man, all good and perfect (Jas. 1:17), let us consider three of His greatest.

THE GREAT GIFT OF HIS SON

"For God so loved the world, that He gave His only begotten Son..." (Jn. 3:16). The greatness of the Son of God, none but the Father is able to reveal and He has done so in Hebrews 1:1-6, presenting to us seven supernal glories of Christ:

He is the future Ruler of the Universe—"the appointed Heir of all things." A universal Potentate is He to be, with the heavens and earth under His reign. This is the Father's declared purpose, to "gather together in one all things in Christ, both which are in heaven, and which are on earth; even in Him" (Eph. 1:10).

He is the past Creator of the Universe—"by whom also He made the worlds." The chief Agent of creation is Christ the Son, "for by Him were all things created, that are in heaven, and that are in earth, visible and invisible...all things were created by Him, and for Him" (Col. 1:16).

He is the Eternal Son of the Highest, very God Himself—"being the effulgence of His glory and the expression of His substance"

(JND Trans.). Every divine attribute of God's moral glory and being, He possesses in its fullness.

He is the Sustainer of the Universe—"upholding all things by the word of His power." He holds the mighty universe together, for "He is before all, and all things subsist together by Him" (Col. 1:17, JND Trans.). Every atom is in His mighty control. "In Him, all things hold together." (*Confraternity Edition*)

He is the great Sin Purger—"when He had by Himself purged our sins." The greatness of sin in God's moral universe He alone could put away to the infinite satisfaction of a holy God, and this He did. "But now once in the end of the ages hath He appeared to put away sin by the sacrifice of Himself" (Heb. 9:26). How great is God's gift of His Son!

He is the Exalted Man in the Glory of Heaven—for He "sat down" [and note where] on the right hand of the Majesty on High." The pinnacle of universal glory is His portion right now. Man gave Him a crown of thorns and a cross; the Father gave Him a crown of glory and a throne (Heb. 2:9).

He is the Coming Saviour-King. He must and will return to earth, for "when He again bringeth in the firstborn into the world He saith, And let all the angels of God worship Him" (Heb. 1:6, ASV)

This One is God's Great Gift to the world—"that whosoever believeth in Him, should not perish but have everlasting life." Great and eternal are the blessings for all who trust Him. "Thanks be unto God for His unspeakable gift" (2 Cor. 9:15).

> *"Of all the gifts Thy love bestows,*
> *Thou Giver of all good!*
> *Not heaven itself a richer knows*
> *Than the Redeemer's blood."* (William Cowper)

THE GREAT GIFT OF HIS SPIRIT

"The love of God is shed abroad in our hearts by the Holy Ghost which is given unto us" (Rom. 5:5). The greatest deed of infamy ever perpetrated by humanity was the slaying of the Son of God. The world united to nail in shame upon the cross, God's Holy One, "the Lord of Glory" (1 Cor. 2:8). Many infamous crimes have been committed and continue to fill human history, revealing the wickedness of the human heart. Yet for the betrayal and murder of God's Son (Acts 7:52), we would think that sudden and eternal destruction from God would have occurred. But no! The God of mercy and grace continues to prove His great love to mankind by sending from heaven another great gift, the Holy Spirit.

Within fifty days of the crucifixion of Christ, the Spirit of God descended from heaven, keeping the promise of the Father (Jn. 14:16, 17, 26) and the promise of the Son (Jn. 16:7). The Father, the omnipresent One (Eph. 4:6) is, as to His abode, in heaven (Mt. 6:9). God the Son, likewise, though omnipresent (Mt. 18:20), as to His abode now, is seated at the right hand of God (Heb. 1:3; 10:12). But the Holy Spirit, also omnipresent, is now as to His abode, dwelling here on earth since the Day of Pentecost.

Two specific revelations concerning His present place in the world are taught in the New Testament. In a corporate aspect, He tabernacles in a structure of living stones (believers in the Lord Jesus Christ), making them the present habitation of God. (Read Eph. 2:18-22; Eph. 4:13-16.) In an individual aspect, He dwells in every child of God! (Read 1 Cor. 6:19.) Blessed condescension of God to send from above His Spirit to indwell His people, greatest gift from above now on the earth!

> *"And all that trust Christ's precious blood,*
> *To them the Spirit is given.*
> *Thou matchless Giver of all good!*
> *Hast sent Him down from heaven.*

THE GREAT GIFT OF HIS SCRIPTURES

"All Scripture is given by inspiration of God" (2 Tim. 3:16). An infallible Book from the hand of God! Here is a divine library of sixty-six books, yet one volume. Written by about forty different men, over a period of 1600 years, many of them never seeing or knowing each other—yet it has a perfect continuity of historical sequence, from the creation to the new heaven and the new earth, from Genesis through Revelation. This supernatural Book reveals the Person and the glory of God. Its supreme purpose is to make us wise unto salvation and that we may be complete to accomplish the will of the Lord in and through our lives (2 Tim. 3:14-17).

These are God's Three Great Gifts to us, each one to be within our hearts (see Eph. 3:17; Gal. 4:6; Ps. 119:11).

God's three great gifts are these from heaven—
His Son, His Spirit, and His Word;
And to our hearts they have been given
To glorify our Lord.

May the possession of God's Son, God's Spirit, and God's Word fill your heart with joy unspeakable through life's journey to the end of your days.

9
The Cup

What perfect submission to the Father's will is shown by the Lord when He said to Peter, "The cup which My Father hath given Me, shall I not drink it?" (Jn. 18:11). The portion of sorrow, suffering and death given Him can only be fully known to God. But we may reverently meditate on it for some blessing and practical instruction in our lives.

1. *Prepared by the Father's wisdom:* In his Pentecost sermon, Peter declared, that though wicked hands had crucified the Lord, it was "by the determinate counsel and foreknowledge of God" (Acts 2:23). Later, he writes that it was "verily foreordained before the foundation of the world" (1 Pet. 1:20). He was the sacrificial Lamb, "without blemish and without spot" given for our redemption. "O the depth of the riches both of the wisdom and knowledge of God" (Rom. 11:33). The cup was prepared in eternity for Him.

2. *Appointed in the Father's love:* The Father loved Him "before the foundation of the world" (Jn. 17:24). He loved Him when on the earth (Jn. 3:35; 5:20). He loved Him in death (Jn. 10:17). The Son of His love knew this cup was offered with His Father's love, for the Son eternally dwells in the bosom of the Father (Jn. 1:18). The cup, with its awful contents, was the appointment from the Father of love!

3. *Designed for the Father's Son:* It is "given Me," said Jesus. Myriads of celestial and terrestrial beings have been created, but this cup was for the Son alone. He "made by Himself the purification of sins" (Heb. 1:3, JND Trans.). "The form of the verb

here—made—had a peculiar reflexive force: 'having done it for Himself.' Though we, as alone the sinners, have the profit, yet the work was done within His own person, without us." Why "for Himself"? He purchased the "Pearl of great price" for Himself (Mt. 13:45-46). The redemption and glorification of His Bride was for Himself (Eph. 5:25-27). The Father's design was to bestow upon His beloved Son everlasting joy and glory through eternal ages (Eph. 3:21; Rev. 11:15).

4. *Accepted for the Father's sake:* "Shall I not drink it?" said the Lord. Did not the Son declare to His Father, "Lo, I come to do Thy will, O God"? (Heb. 10:7, 9). To His disciples He said, "My meat is to do the will of Him that sent Me, and to finish His work" (Jn. 4:34). In His agony in Gethsemane, as the cup pressed nearer to His soul, we hear Him say, "Nevertheless, not My will but Thine be done" (Lk. 22:42) as He pours out His burdened heart to the Father. Perfect submission! For the Father's sake, He goes to the Cross and drains the bitter cup (Jn. 17:4).

> *"Death and the curse were in our cup,*
> *O Christ! 'twas full for Thee!*
> *But Thou hast drained the last dark drop,*
> *'Tis empty now for me.*
> *That bitter cup—love drank it up;*
> *Left but the love for me."* (Ann Ross Cousin)

Beloved, has not the Father prepared *our* cup in His wisdom? Appointed it in His love? Designed it for His child? Shall we not accept it for the Father's sake and glory? Ours can never be compared with His cup that He drank! Why should it then be hard to say, "Nevertheless, not my will, but Thine be done." From our Saviour's example may we truly learn that that *the greatest mission in the world is submission*!

10
At Home

Following the Rapture and the Judgment Seat of Christ, who can imagine the joy of entering into the Father's House according to the promise of the Saviour in John 14:3. It is the Lord Jesus Christ who alone reveals the truth concerning the Father's house; only He could do this (see Jn. 13:3). There are some blessed facts revealed by Him in John 14:1-6 about this Home:

1. *Its reality is revealed:* "If it were not so I would have told you" (v. 2). His words assure us of the reality of it. Also my faith in God assures me (v. 1). My faith in Christ assures me. And my faith in the Word of God and its many promises of that future glory assures me of its reality.

2. *Its locality is revealed:* It is "a place" (vv. 2-3). Heaven is not only a condition to enjoy, but a place as well—"the secret place of the Most High" (Ps. 91:1). Paul called it "the third heaven" and "paradise" (2 Cor. 12:2-4). It is the place where my heavenly Father dwells, my Saviour and His holy angels (Mt. 18:10); it is the place where departed saints are (see 2 Cor. 5:1-8; Phil. 1:23). The Hebrews long ago believed that the highest pinnacle of the universe was God's heaven. But we know it is God's heart.

3. *Its felicity is revealed:* "Let not your heart be troubled," said the Saviour. He knew the felicity and blessedness of His Father's home and its eternal compensation for the believer when there. See what is *not* there: no tears, death, sorrow, crying, or pain (Rev. 21:4). And see what *is* there: it is a home of perfect love (Jn. 17:26); a home of perfect rest (Heb. 4:9); a home of perfect joy (Ps. 16:11); and a home of perfect fellowship (1 Jn. 1:3; Rev. 21:3).

4. *Its immensity is revealed:* There are "many mansions" (v. 2). Who can count the multitude of saints who will be there? They are "a great multitude" (Rev. 7:9). The house will be filled (Lk. 14:23). The children will be many and God and His Christ will be satisfied with the results of redemption's work (Heb. 2:13; Isa. 53:11; Eph. 1:4).

5. *Its permanency is revealed:* What are these "mansions" (v. 2)? This word in the Greek text has the suggestion of permanency. It is an abiding place. God is the Architect and Builder (Heb. 11:10; 13:14). "And I will dwell in the house of the Lord forever," said the Psalmist (Ps. 23:6).

6. *Its imminency is revealed:* "And if I go and prepare a place for you, I will come again and receive you unto Myself, that where I am, there you may be also" (v. 3). The Christian is to be expecting the Lord to come and "to wait for God's Son from heaven" (1 Thess. 1:10). It is important to realize that the first definite event of prophecy is the removal of the Church from the earth, before the fulfillment of other prophecies yet to come. All indications of the approaching climax to history are being seen today in the world. Present-day conditions among the nations and in Israel clearly are marching forward to the drastic events of judgment to come on the earth, which will follow after the removal of the Church to heaven; but the Christian looks for the Lord to come for His saints before final prophecy is fulfilled.

7. *Its accessibility is revealed:* "Jesus saith unto him, I am the Way, the Truth and the Life; no man cometh unto the Father, but by Me" (Jn. 14:6). The Way is a Person—Christ Himself. He is also the exclusive Way: "No man cometh unto the Father, but by Me," He said.

> *How blest a home! The Father's house!*
> *There love divine doth rest;*
> *What else could satisfy the hearts of those*
> *In Jesus blest?*
> *His home made ours—the Father's love*
> *Our heart's full portion given,*
> *The portion of the firstborn Son,*
> *The full delight of heaven.* (J. A. Trench)

11
My Father's Name

What contrasting claims are revealed in John 5:43—the claims of Christ and Antichrist! One comes in His "Father's Name" and the other "in his own name" to Israel. One is the Father's representative to do His will (Jn. 6:37-38; 10:25) and the other represents "the great red dragon" (Rev. 12 & 13). With great sorrow of heart the Saviour condemned His people, saying, "Ye received Me not." What appalling retribution will be Israel's in the day of their future political crisis! They will take to their hearts the Antichrist and cover him with praises, expecting him to satisfy their political and religious ambitions (Dan. 9:27; 11:36-39). Instead of "the Good Shepherd" they will prefer "the Foolish Shepherd" who in cruelty will be God's chastening instrument upon them in the closing days (Zech. 11:15-17). What a revelation of the depravity of the human heart is this! But what did the Saviour mean by saying, "I am come in My Father's Name"?

1. *He came with His Father's image in His person:* "He that hath seen Me hath seen the Father," said Jesus, "image of the invisible God" (Col. 1:15). Every divine attribute of the Godhead resided in Him when He walked on earth. He was and is eternally "the brightness of His glory, and the express image of His person" (Heb. 1:3). Yet, blinded by Satan, they knew Him not and this is true of many today! (2 Cor. 4:3-6). Nevertheless, He was the outshining image of the Father!

"Image of the Infinite unseen, whose Being none can know;
Brightness of light no eye has seen—God's love revealed below." (J. C.)

2. *He came with His Father's love in His heart:* "God is love" (1 Jn. 4:8) and the perfect manifestation of His love was revealed in and by the Son. "In this was manifested the love of God toward us, because that God sent His only begotten Son into the world, that we might live through Him. Herein is love, not that we loved God, but that He loved us, and sent His Son - the propitiation for our sins" (1 Jn. 4:9-10). The fullness of the Father's love dwelt in the heart of the Son, "for in Him dwelleth all the fullness of the Godhead bodily" (Col. 2:9). How blind were His people and how blind many are today!

> *"Life, life of love poured out, fragrant and holy!*
> *Life, 'mid rude thorns of earth, stainless and sweet!*
> *Life, whence God's face of love, glorious but lowly,*
> *Shines forth to bow us, Lord, low at Thy feet!"* (F. Allaben)

3. *He came with His Father's words upon His lips:* "I speak *to the world* those things which I have heard of Him" (Jn. 8:26-27). Words which He had heard thru eternal ages when dwelling in the bosom of His Father! "As the Father hath taught me, I speak these things" (Jn. 8:28; 14:10). When He spoke in Nazareth they "all bare Him witness, and wondered at the gracious words which proceeded out of His mouth" (Lk. 4:22). Men were compelled to declare, "Never man spake like this Man!" (Jn. 7:46). His lips "were like lilies, dropping sweet smelling myrrh" (S. of S. 5:13). With divine authority He taught the people (Mt. 7:29), and yet they did not esteem the words of His mouth more than their necessary food (Job 23:12). Do we? May our prayer be:

> *"Lord, speak to me that I may speak*
> *In living echoes of Thy tone."* (F. R. Havergal)

4. *He came with His Father's works in His hands:* "The Son can do nothing of Himself, but what He seeth the Father do: for what things soever He doeth, that also doeth the Son likewise" (Jn. 5:19-20). What blessed hands of ministry were His! Always filled with the works of His Father, healing the sick, touching the leper, opening blind eyes, giving speech to the dumb, hearing to the deaf, and life to the dead! Who can begin to measure the infinite power of His hands when He worked among men?

"I do always those things that please Him" (Jn. 8:29). The Father's perfect Servant—yet confessing, "the Father that dwelleth in Me, He doeth the works" (Jn. 14:10). Blessed mystery!

Yet His work was not completed until those blessed hands were nailed to the Cross of shame and suffering! Those priceless hands ("as gold rings set with the beryl," S. of S. 5:14) were pierced through with cruel nails by the hands of wicked men, the ones He came to save! Those hands are for ever scarred and will be the eternal evidence of the Father's work of redemption through His beloved Son for a world of sinners lost! The saints in glory will ever sing their song of worship, love, praise and honor to the Lamb that was slain (Rev. 5:9-10).

> "Thy wounds, Thy wounds, Lord Jesus,
> Those deep, deep wounds will tell
> The sacrifice that frees us,
> From self, and death, and hell!
> These link Thee once forever
> With all who own Thy grace;
> No hands these wounds can sever,
> No hands these scars efface." (C. A. H.)

5. *He came with His Father's glory before His eyes*· From the moment He left the Father's home above, to the consummation of His death upon the Cross, the Father's glory was ever before Him. "No man hath seen God at any time; the only begotten Son, which is in the bosom of the Father, He hath declared Him" (Jn. 1:18). In complete and perfect self-effacement the Son testified - "I seek not Mine own will, but the will of the Father which hath sent Me" (Jn. 5:30). The pure motive of His heart in representing His Father was - "I seek not Mine own glory" (Jn. 8:50). When the Cross, with its suffering and shame was imminent, He said, "Father, glorify Thy Name" (Jn. 12:28). In perfection He kept the Father's glory ever before Him to the end!

When redemption was fully accomplished and the Father's will for Him on earth was consummated, He lifts His heart and voice to the loving Father and says: "I have glorified Thee on the earth: I have finished the work which Thou gavest Me to do"

(Jn. 17:4). He manifested in fullness His Father's Name on the earth. Oh, that we had some measure of the Father's glory before our eyes like the Son of His love!

> *"Brightness of eternal glory,*
> *Shall Thy praise unuttered lie?*
> *Who would hush the heaven-sent story,*
> *Of the Lamb who came to die?*
>
> *Came from Godhead's fullest glory*
> *Down to Calvary's depth of woe,*
> *Now on high, we bow before Thee;*
> *Streams of praises ceaseless flow!"* (R. Robinson)

What a tragic sadness is before Israel and its people to whom He said, "Ye received *Me* not!" Yet what eternal gladness is before those of whom it is recorded, "As many as received Him, to them gave He power to become the sons of God, even to them that believe on His Name" (Jn. 1:12). Our own hearts can ask the searching question, if we will: How much do I appreciate the One who came in His Father's Name, bearing His Father's image, possessing the Father's love, speaking the Father's words, doing the Father's will and work, and manifesting always His Father's glory?

May our brief meditation produce a salutary effect on our hearts, consciences, and lives for the glory of our blessed Lord.

Part Two
The Son of God's Love

12
His Riches, Our Riches

"For ye know the grace of our Lord Jesus Christ, that, though He was rich, yet for your sakes He became poor, that ye through His poverty might be rich" (2 Cor. 8:9).

Who can fathom the unsearchable riches of Christ? The riches of His past eternal glory, who can declare? He left the riches of the Father's glory above for earth's unequaled poverty. The poverty of His birth, can it be understood? The great Creator, worthy of earth's highest homage, found only a lowly cattle shed for His entrance here. Then think of the poverty of His life. He, the Creator and Sustainer of all things (Heb. 1:2-3), possessed nothing of this world when on earth. Why then do we grasp after so much?

Yet deeper, deeper still, is the poverty of His death. Forsaken and rejected by men; forsaken and rejected by God when on the Cross for you and me. None shall ever understand the depths of His poverty there! Hear Him cry, "I looked for some to take pity, but there was none; and for comforters, but I found none" (Ps. 69:20). The heavens shut out their light, and impenetrable darkness wrapped His holy soul, as God, His God, hid His face from His beloved Son as He sank down into the depths of the Cross! In mire where there was no standing (Ps. 69:2), we hear Him cry in sorrow, "Thou hast laid Me in the lowest pit, in darkness, in the deeps. Thy wrath lieth hard upon Me, and Thou hast afflicted Me with all Thy waves" (Ps. 88:6-7). Who can fathom the depth of His poverty there—depths into which He descended

57

for you and me, to obtain our eternal redemption (Heb. 9:12-15)?

Nevertheless, through His poverty, the saints are rich! Men of the world, according to natural reasoning, are made rich by accumulating wealth; but here is One who makes us rich by going into poverty! Paradoxical, you say? Yes, but true! Let us see how the Lord Jesus Christ, by leaving His riches in glory, has made His people rich, bringing unto them His own riches by grace alone. What are the riches that now are ours?

1. *The Riches of His Grace:* God saves sinners by grace and there is no other way of salvation offered to men (see Eph. 2:8-9 and Acts 4:12). One has said, "Saving grace is the limitless, unrestrained love of God for the lost, with the exact and unchangeable demands of His own righteousness met through the sacrificial death of Christ." God sets aside all human merit, providing salvation through sovereign grace alone, lest any man would boast of a salvation through the merit of his own strength (Rom. 3:9; Rom. 11:32; Gal. 3:22).

Beyond saving us by grace, the apostle James writes, "He giveth *more* grace" (Jas. 4:6). Through grace alone He keeps those who are saved, continuing to exercise unmerited favor toward the saved ones, securing our safekeeping forever, for we are said to stand in grace (Rom. 5:2; 1 Pet. 5:12). What a blessed place of security: standing in grace.

Yet for all our paths of life, that we may live for His eternal glory, He ministers grace sufficient for every need. Do we know the riches of His grace as we ought? One of God's greatest servants suffered a severe testing, "a thorn in the flesh, a messenger of Satan," which, with its severity, caused him to entreat God three times for its removal. He was thrice denied and then was offered an even greater blessing than the removal of his trial. "My grace is sufficient for thee," was the Lord's reply to Paul (2 Cor. 12:9). The apostle declares that the physical disability proved to be a spiritual blessing, twice acknowledging the wisdom of God in allowing it, "lest I be exalted above measure" (2 Cor. 12:7). Far better than the removal of the thorn was the supply of grace from the Lord to bear it! Do we always want the removal of our thorns? Or do we appreciate, in the midst of varied trials, the riches of His grace? It is this that enables us to bear every burden and trial that it pleases Him to permit in our lives.

2. *The Riches of His Strength:* Paul's trial revealed conscious weakness; lack of strength to carry the great burdens of the work entrusted to him. But he learned that even this is a spiritual advantage: "My strength is made perfect in weakness," declares the Lord (2 Cor. 12:9). Note the joyful triumph which rings in Paul's response: "Most gladly therefore will I rather boast in my weaknesses, that the power of Christ may rest upon me. Wherefore I take pleasure in weaknesses, in insults, in necessities, in persecutions, in straits, for Christ; for when I am weak, then am I powerful" (2 Cor. 12:9-10, JND Trans.).

How much of this do we know? How can we? One scriptural way, which even the weakest saint may prove, is to wait upon the Lord! "They that wait upon the Lord shall renew their strength...they shall walk and not faint" (Isa. 40:31). The prophet had previously assured that God "giveth power to the faint and to them that have no might, He increaseth strength!" So today, the ministry of waiting upon God, greatly neglected, imparts to the believer the riches of His strength! Read the wonderful story of Jehoshaphat in 2 Chronicles 20:1-30, and note in particular the words of the king in verse 12.

Another channel of His strength is the Word of God. How aptly is this illustrated for us in Daniel 10:7-11, where the prophet, in utter weakness, is prostrated on the ground before the celestial visitor from glory! Daniel's companions all fled to hide from the angel. Daniel writes, "There remained no strength in me," but the touch of the angel's hand and the encouraging words impart strength to him, enabling Daniel to stand. "As he spoke this word unto me, I stood trembling." Surely this reminds us that the Lord's strength is ministered to us in our weakness, through His precious Word.

"Thy words were found; and I did eat them; and Thy word was unto me the joy and rejoicing of mine heart," wrote Jeremiah (Jer. 15:16). Those were days of great weakness in Judah and Jerusalem, causing God's servant to give expression to great lamentation and sorrow because of the condition of His people. The Psalmist uttered, "Wherewithal shall a young man cleanse his way? by taking heed thereto according to Thy Word"

(Ps. 119:9). Surely these are days of great moral and spiritual weakness, testing the saints as well as the whole race of mankind in these perilous times. Let us find our strength in the precious Word of God.

In this manner, fellowship with God will produce spiritual strength and godliness of life, manifesting that our God is able to strengthen His children and sustain them to stand for Him, even though the power of the enemy is all around.

Such strength of character and testimony was seen in Joseph, a man who lived the greater part of his life in Egypt, surrounded with idolatry and worldly power. Yet of Joseph, his father said before departing this life, "His bow abideth firm, and the arms of his hands are supple, by the hands of the mighty One of Jacob" (Gen. 49:24, JND). May the Lord grant us to know each day what our riches are; proving that we avail ourselves of the riches of His strength (see Eph. 6:10-18).

THE RICHES OF HIS PEACE

How exhaustless are the riches of our Lord Jesus Christ! He continues to minister them, saying, "My peace I leave with you, My peace I give unto you; not as the world giveth, give I unto you. Let not your heart be troubled, neither let it be afraid" (Jn. 14:27). The riches of My peace! World peace? No! It is not from the world, neither for the world; but only from the Lord and for His own. Every believer can enjoy this.

We have first, peace *with* God. "Therefore being justified by faith, we have peace with God through our Lord Jesus Christ" (Rom. 5:1). How blessed to be reconciled to God and enjoy peace with Him: "Be careful about nothing; but in everything, by prayer and supplication with thanksgiving, let your requests be made known unto God; and the peace of God, which surpasses all understanding, shall guard your hearts and your thoughts by Christ Jesus" (Phil. 4:6-7, JND).

An artist once painted his conception of peace in a weary world like ours. It merited the first prize in the competition for which is was entered. He portrayed a violent storm on the edge of the sea near a rugged and rocky coast. He graphically painted the waves lashing against the lofty rocks. Then, in a cleft in the rock, he pictured a bird sitting on its nest, sweetly singing its song of praise to the Creator above! That to him was a true description of peace in a world of sorrow and storm. Does not this illustrate the peace the believer has today? His peace!

"While I hear life's rugged billows, Peace, peace is mine!
Why suspend my harp on willows? Peace, peace is mine!
I may sing, with Christ beside me, tho' a thousand ills betide me,
Safely hath He sworn to guide me! Peace, peace is mine!" (J. D. Smith)

THE RICHES OF HIS JOY

"I have spoken these things unto you that My joy might remain in you, and that your joy might be full" (Jn. 15:11). It has been said that we never read of Christ ever laughing. Yes, He truly was "a Man of sorrows and acquainted with grief." Nevertheless, He possessed real joy. The reality of His joy was an integral part of His experience on earth, and a joy that He desires us to experience also. What was His joy? Can we have it?

Listen to a divine conversation between the Son of God and His Father, recorded in Psalm 40:7-8, revealing His joy on earth: "Then said I, behold, I come, in the volume of this book it is written of Me; to do Thy good pleasure, My God, is My delight, and Thy law is within My heart" (JND Trans.). His joy on earth was to do His Father's will. Cannot this be our joy, too?

This joy He experienced at Sychar's well (Jn. 4), as He led a sinful woman into the knowledge of Himself, giving her living water. When the disciples offered Him food to eat, He replied, "I have meat to eat that ye know not of." Upon further questioning, He told them, "My [food] is to do the will of Him that sent Me, and to finish His work" (Jn. 4:34). Seeking the lost ones was a source of His joy on earth and should be ours. Is it?

When He faced the rejection of the nation of Israel—the rulers and elders refusing His Messianic claims—though left with but a few unlearned disciples, yet we read: "In that hour Jesus rejoiced in spirit, and said, I thank Thee, O Father, Lord of heaven and earth, that Thou hast hid these things from the wise and prudent, and hast revealed them unto babes; even so, Father, for so it seemed good in Thy sight" (Lk. 10:21). This was His joy—

teaching His weak and ignorant followers the Father's will, ministering with constant patience His precious Word. Is this our joy? What a ministry is needed that will, in patience, seek to edify the saints today, weak as they may be, by bringing to them the precious truths of the Word of God!

THE RICHES OF HIS LOVE

"As the Father hath loved Me, so have I loved you; continue ye in My love" (Jn. 15:9-10). We proclaim to the sinner God's love, as declared in John 3:16. But above this is the love of Christ for His saints. The Apostle Paul prayed for the saints of Ephesus: "That Christ may dwell in your hearts by faith; that ye, being rooted and grounded in love, may be able to comprehend with all saints what is the breadth, and length, and depth, and height; and to know (the experiential enjoyment of acquired knowledge) the love of Christ which passeth knowledge, that ye might be filled with all the fullness of God" (Eph. 3:17-19).

The Lord will always love His own, you say! True, but do we not realize how much *more* He wants us to enjoy His love? This is dependent on our obedience to Him and His Word: "If ye keep My commandments, ye shall abide in My love." In John 14:21, the Saviour said, "He that hath My commandments, and keepeth them, he it is that loveth Me: and he that loveth Me shall be loved of My Father, and I will love him, and will manifest Myself to him."

There are two Greek words for love in the New Testament: *agapao* and *phileo*. The first is used by the Lord Jesus as a command in Matthew 5:44, "Love your enemies," and also in John 15:12, "Love one another." Its usage properly denotes a love founded in admiration, veneration, esteem, to be kindly disposed to one, to wish one well. One has said, "It signifies the love as the settled disposition of the person (necessarily resulting in activity) rather than as an emotion."

The second word, *phileo,* signifies the love of friendship, and implies attractiveness in the one loved. It is translated "to have affection for" of "to be attached to." The noun, *philos,* is "friend"; another derivation is "kiss." In this way we see that love as an emotion cannot be commanded, but must be promoted by some attraction in the one loved.

This is singularly used but a few times in the New Testament, of which the following scriptures are an example. It is used concerning Lazarus of Bethany in John 11:3, "Lord, behold, he whom Thou lovest (art attached to) is sick." When "Jesus wept" at the grave of Lazarus, the only occasion that it is said He literally shed silent tears, "The Jews therefore said, Behold how He loved (or was attached) to him" (Jn. 11:36).

John the Apostle has it written of himself in John 20:2, when Mary ran from the sepulcher to "Simon Peter, and to the other disciple, to whom Jesus was attached" (JND Trans.). Surely we recognize that there was cause for this special attachment to John by the Lord Jesus. Then again in John 16:27, we have significant words from the Lord, "For the Father Himself has affection (*phileo*) for Me." Surely we can safely conclude that some attractiveness in the Lord's people will increase His love for them.

Other Scriptures in our New Testament, though few, clearly indicate that, if in our love and obedience to the Lord and His Word, we seek to manifest our love to Him, we shall then be able to partake more and more of the riches of His love for us. Surely we recognize this is contingent on our obedient love to Him. May the Spirit of God make the experimental knowledge of His love known more and more.

THE RICHES OF HIS GLORY

"Father, I will that they also, whom Thou hast given Me be with Me where I am; that they may behold My glory which Thou gavest Me" (Jn. 17:24), prayed the Saviour. There never has been and never will be an equal to the unselfish love that the Saviour manifests for us in expressing such a desire! His great heart pleads for His people to share with Him the glory the Father will bestow.

Note John 17:22, and hear the Saviour tell the Father, "And the glory which Thou hast given Me, I have given them." What a Giver! Withholding nothing from His saints! His grace, His strength, His peace, His joy, His love, and now His glory is for us. Incomparable unselfishness—all that we might be rich! "The Spirit Himself witnesseth with our spirit, that we are the children of God; and if children, then heirs; heirs of God, and joint-heirs with Christ; if so be that we suffer with Him, that we may be also glorified together. For I reckon that the sufferings of this present time are not worthy to be compared with the glory which shall be revealed in us" (Rom. 8:16-18).

Yet we must recognize a solemn fact, that though we shall share in His future glory as His children, yet our measure of participation in it involves our present faithfulness in suffering for Him on earth. "If we suffer, we shall also reign with Him; if we deny Him, He also will deny us" (2 Tim. 2:12). The Apostle Peter reminds us throughout his first epistle that it is from "sufferings to glory" we must go. Every child of God will share that glory in some measure, but how much will be yours and mine? We must not forget that "one star differeth from another in glory," so that in our present responsibility to Him, we should be faithfully bearing His reproach, to be the worthy participators of His glory which He will share in that day of eternal reward.

Let us remember that His glory is not only in the Father's house of blessing above, but also to be manifested in the millennial kingdom on earth. It will also be manifested through the ages of eternity, abiding in its fullness forever. How this should stir our hearts today to seek by His grace to be faithfully living for Him in this present scene of testing and trial. Though the trials may be great, yet He has said through His servant, Peter, "That the trial of your faith, being much more precious than of gold that perisheth, though it be tried with fire, might be found unto praise and honor and glory at the appearing of Jesus Christ" (1 Pet. 1:7). How encouraging are these words, for our trial is "but for a moment," yet our glory is an "exceeding and eternal weight of glory" (2 Cor. 4:15-18).

Much more could be added, but surely these truths are sufficient to enable us to realize that our Lord Jesus Christ, through His deep poverty, has brought abundant riches to us: His grace, His strength, His peace, His love, and His glory! This brings us into agreement with the words of the apostle in 2 Corinthians 8:9, "For ye know the grace of our Lord Jesus Christ, that, though He was rich, yet for your sakes He became poor, that ye through His poverty might be rich."

13
The Most Unforgettable Character

There have been three historic occasions written in the history of the United States, calling to remembrance certain deeds of heroism and tragedy, concerning persons not to be forgotten:

The Defense of the Alamo. In 1835, the people of Texas, then a part of the Republic of Mexico, revolted in order to annex with the United States. In 1836, Santa Anna, a Mexican general, was sent with an army of several thousand men to crush the revolution. He was, for a time, successful, but it was the heroic defense of the old fort, the Alamo, at San Antonio, by 183 Texans, that inspired the people to final victory in their efforts of resistance. A little band of 183 endured a siege of thirteen days, and when all but six of the garrison had been killed, the Mexicans took the fort by storm. The six survivors were ordered to be shot at once by Santa Anna. The war cry of Texas then became, "Remember the Alamo."

The Spanish American War. In the city of Charleston, South Carolina, near the harbor, can be seen the capstan of the U.S.S. Maine, a warship that presumably was destroyed by the Spaniards in the harbor of Havana, Cuba, with the loss of 266 men through an external explosion the night of February 15, 1898. On one side of the capstan is written the battle cry of the Spanish American War, "Remember the Maine."

World War II. In the early dawn of Sunday, December 7, 1941, a Japanese squadron commanded by Captain Fuchida (who by God's great grace has since been saved), made a successful and devastating attack on the naval fleet at anchor in Pearl Harbor,

Hawaii. This abrupt and pre-meditated attack precipitated the entrance of the United States into the war, with the battle cry, "Remember Pearl Harbor."

These historic events have been recorded in history to remind succeeding generations of the heroic and tragic deaths of brave characters who have preceded us; yet with the passing of time, how prone humanity is to forget them. Nevertheless, on the pages of human history has been written the life and death of one Person who indeed is the most unforgettable.

THE MOST UNFORGETTABLE CHARACTER

This One is none other than the Lord Jesus Christ, the Son of the Living God, who above and beyond all human deeds of heroism, is and ever will be the most unforgettable character of all history. Centuries ago, in the solitude of the Upper Room, with a handful of trembling disciples, He faced the greatest of all conflicts the earth has ever witnessed—the battle of Calvary! The consequences involved were not of a mere temporal character alone, but eternal in their implications. The suffering entailed was beyond all human comprehension, as His soul marched to that inevitable crisis of the Cross.

It was not the deliverance of a few men that was involved, nor even the deliverance of one nation, but provision for the redemption of the human race. It was to be the decisive factor in the conflict of the ages, to defeat the forces of sin, hell, and Satan, that He might deliver the captives for the glory of God's grace and the eternal blessing of the souls of men. He, one lone Man, was to die for all (read 2 Cor. 5:14-15). How could it be? His death was of such value that it would be for every man. There has been no equal to such a sacrifice as this, and there never will be. Then can He be forgotten? Shall the scroll of time erase from memory such a deed as Calvary's Cross where the Son of God died to redeem us?

REMEMBER ME

In that Upper Room, on the last occasion before His death, that blessed, lowly Man of Sorrows instituted a practice for His followers that would perpetuate His memory in their hearts down through the era of Christianity. He followed an Oriental custom both in Israel and other lands of the East, taking bread and wine and giving them to His disciples to do in like manner, saying, "This do in remembrance of Me."

It was once the custom of friends to send food and wine to console relatives at their mourning feasts (read Jer. 16:7, JND Trans.; note also Job 42:11). Thus our blessed Lord used "the breaking of bread" and "the cup of consolation" whereby His precious Person and redeeming work shall never be forgotten.

Centuries have passed since the institution of this memorial feast and the finished work of His Cross, but there has never failed to be, through the centuries, a remembrance of the blessed Saviour. The powers of darkness and Satan have manifested themselves in hatred and persecution against His Church, but there has been among His people the faithful remembrance of their Lord, according to His request.

To this very day throughout the world, companies of God's children can be found, whether large or small, who in obedience to His request, acknowledge Him as the most unforgettable character. They "break the bread" and "drink the cup" in loving memory of Him. Are you among the number? Their heart language is expressed by the bride in the Song of Solomon 1:4, saying: "We will remember Thy love."

We should say, as recorded in Isaiah 26:8, "The desire of our soul is to Thy Name, and to the remembrance of Thee" He is the most unforgettable character we have met!

> *"Gethsemane, can I forget,*
> *Or there Thy conflict see,*
> *Thine agony and blood-like sweat,*
> *And not remember Thee?*
>
> *"When to the cross I turn mine eyes,*
> *And rest on Calvary,*
> *O Lamb of God, my sacrifice,*
> *I must remember Thee."*   (James Montgomery)

THE MOST UNFORGETTABLE CHARACTER IN HEAVEN

We will always remember Him! In the day of heaven's glory,

when He shall be "in the midst of the throne," we shall sing, "Thou art worthy to take the book...for Thou wast slain, and hast redeemed us to God by Thy blood" (read Rev. 5:6-10).

May the Spirit of God enlarge our appreciation and apprehension of this One who—in time and eternity—is the most unforgettable character indeed.

14
We Know Him

"We know Him." Only a triplet of words in 1 John 2:3, nine letters in all, each word a distinct syllable that can be uttered by a single effort of the voice, yet the *summa cum laude* of Christian education! John always presents the Person of Christ. In his Gospel he says to the world: "You need Him!" To the family of God, he writes, "You need Him!" And to the Jew, Gentile and Church in Revelation he again declares, "You need Him!"

More than seminaries, schools, conferences, or convocations, we need the Person of Christ. On the Emmaus road of doubt, despair, discouragement and disillusionment, we read that "Jesus Himself drew near" (Lk. 24:15). From "Moses and all the prophets, He expounded unto them in all the Scriptures, the things concerning Himself" (Lk. 24:27). At the close of that first resurrection day, the Great Shepherd re-gathered His disciples and "Jesus Himself stood in the midst" (Lk. 24:36). They were again around Him.

Beloved, by the Holy Spirit we have been brought to a Person—"we know Him." It is true Jesus said, "No man knoweth the Son, but the Father" (Mt. 11:27) and as one servant of God wrote: "There is that both in the life and death of Christ which God alone can comprehend. Our part is to stand with unshod feet and adoring hearts, as we gaze at this great mystery" God manifest in the flesh, not attempting to define what is indefinable, or gauge what is incomprehensible to creature minds. Nevertheless, John by the Spirit writes: "We know Him." God in His Word has revealed some great glories of His Son for

69

our knowledge and blessing, such as He writes in Hebrews 1:1-6 describing them to us. Meditate on these:

1. *He is the future Ruler of the universe:* The "appointed Heir of all things" (Eph. 1:10). Who can estimate the vastness of this rulership! Let us worshipfully say from our hearts in gratitude and praise, that "We know Him."

2. *He is the Creator of the worlds:* "By whom also He made the worlds." (See Jn. 1:3; Col. 1:16; Heb. 11:3.) Men vainly seek to discover the origin of the universe, but each believer knows his or her Creator and can say, "We know Him."

3. *He is the Brightness of God's glory:* All divine attributes of God dwell in the Person of Christ and the moral glories of His being. (See Jn. 12:45; 14:9.) Though far beyond our limited comprehension, yet in humble adoration we say: "We know Him" (Col. 1:19; 2:9).

4. *He is the Sustainer of the universe:* "Upholding all things by the word of His power," for "by Him all things consist [hold together]" (Col. 1:17). We ourselves are safe in His mighty, omnipotent hands. (See Jn. 10:28.) Why? Because "We know Him." Hallelujah!

5. *He is the great Sin Purger:* "By Himself He purged our sins." This is how we came to know Him. We received a Person—Him! (Jn. 1:12). He took our sins away. Then we began to say the precious truth: "We know Him!"

6. *He is the exalted Man in the glory:* He "sat down on the right hand of the Majesty on high." He is truly Man—the God Man—the Man, Christ Jesus (Ps. 110:1; Heb. 1:13). Not earthly glory was given Him, but heavenly glory! And we can still say: "We know Him."

7. *He is the coming King:* "He bringeth again the firstbegotten into the world…" He is coming again! Will He be a stranger to us? Never—"we know Him"! Even now we say, "Even so, come, Lord Jesus."

We would earnestly pray that the Holy Spirit will raise up Christ-centered ministry that will restore the value of His Person to His people! Then it will be possible to say and prove the words of John 20:20, "Then were the disciples glad when they saw the Lord."

15
Three Cheers

Encouraging to the heart of a believer are the three good cheers of the Lord Jesus:

1. *The good cheer of His pardon:* "Son, be of good cheer; thy sins be forgiven thee" (Mt. 9:2). The words forgiveness and remission means to remove, release, send away; to lose something! What does God do when He forgives *all* our sin (1 Jn. 1:7)? He puts them out of reach (Ps. 103:12); out of sight (read Micah 7:19); then He puts them out of mind (Jer. 31:34; Heb. 10:17).

What a joy to have all our sins gone from His reach, His sight, His memory! No wonder the Psalmist wrote, "Blessed (happy) is he (or she) whose transgression is forgiven" (Ps. 32:1). What an eternal blessedness to know the good cheer of His pardon.

2. *The good cheer of His power:* "In the world ye shall have tribulation: but be of good cheer; I have overcome the world" (Jn. 16:33). Though eternally forgiven, we face a threefold enemy: the world, the flesh, and the devil!

The danger of the world is described in 1 John 2:15-17; yet the apostle reveals the victory over it in 1 John 5:4-5. The same blessed One who forgave us our sins, is the Victor over the world! And "who is he that overcometh the world, but he that believeth that Jesus is the Son of God."

Concerning the flesh, surely we must agree with Paul: "I know that in me (that is, in my flesh), dwelleth no good thing" (Rom. 7:18). Paul found the secret of victory again in the Victor (Rom. 7:24-25). Read it.

As to the devil, do not minimize his strength! But remember

71

"greater is He that is in you, than he that is in the world" (1 Jn. 4:4). Read the words of Revelation 12:11 and remember the Saviour overcame the adversary by the Word of God (Mt. 4:1-11). The Word of God is an effective sword (Eph. 6:17; Heb. 4:12). Constant occupation of the heart with Christ will always prove the good cheer of His power.

3. *The good cheer of His presence:* "Be of good cheer; it is I; be not afraid" (Mt. 14:27). What a demonstration of the Lord's omnipotence when He walked on the waves toward His disciples that dark night, as if on a solid pavement! (Read Mt. 14:22-33.) In their desperate situation, the disciples heard His voice and experienced the good cheer of His presence! So can we today in every storm of life.

We have them: trials, darkness, adversities, fear. Yet He has promised, "Fear not: for I have redeemed thee, I have called thee by thy name; thou art Mine. When thou passest through the waters, I will be with thee" (Isa. 43:1-2). How many other promises there are in His Word assuring us as He has said, "I will never leave thee, nor forsake thee" (Heb. 13:5-6). Then let us prove the good cheer of His presence always!

And what of the final trial, the exit of life? This passage is inevitable normally to each of us (Heb. 9:27). Yet we still hear Him say, "Be of good cheer, it is I, be not afraid." Like the Psalmist in Psalm 23:4, we can have composure, saying, "I will walk," not panic. Also I can have confidence: "*through* the valley." And I can have courage: "fear no evil." Best of all, I shall have the good cheer of His presence, saying, "for Thou art with me." His comfort will be mine: "Thy rod and Thy staff they comfort me." Surely we will be able to say with Paul, "We are confident,…and willing rather to be absent from the body, and to be present with the Lord" (2 Cor. 5:8). "With Christ, it is far better." To the end of life we have His good cheer, yes, the good cheer of His presence.

> *"Amid the trials which I meet,*
> *Amid the thorns that pierce my feet,*
> *One thought remains supremely sweet,*
> *Thou thinkest, Lord, of me!"*   (Edward Mund)

16
The Great Attraction

In these five Scripture portions—Luke 2:15-16; John 1:35-39; 12:32-33; 19:35-42; and Acts 7:55-56—we see various ways in which individuals were attracted to Christ. They have their application for our hearts today that we may be drawn closer to Him. C. H. Mackintosh wrote: "The Person of Christ is the perfect object for the heart." How true and important this is. Let us note the above incidents for our encouragement:

1. *Some were attracted to Christ by His birth:* The angelic "birth announcement" by the heavenly hosts impelled the shepherds to say "one to another, Let us now go even unto Bethlehem, and see this thing which is come to pass." There they "found...the Babe lying in a manger." What a priceless privilege was theirs, to be the first to gaze upon "Emmanuel...God with us" on the very day of His birth! These humble shepherds honored the mighty Creator when born, while all the world lay in darkness and ignorance of His entrance into this earthly scene.

Simeon later held Him in his arms and gazed on his salvation. Anna, the prophetess, came into the temple to contribute her thanksgiving for Him and told of Him to all who were looking for redemption in Jerusalem. The wise men came from afar to worship Him who was "born King of the Jews." How much there is for us to meditate on from the Word of God in relation to the Lord of glory coming to earth to be manifested in the flesh. Wondrous mystery! (1 Tim. 3:16).

2. *Some were attracted to Christ by His walk:* It was when John the Baptist was "looking upon Jesus as He walked, he saith,

73

Behold the Lamb of God." These words attracted Andrew and John to Christ and "they followed Jesus." The perfect walk of the Lamb of God upon the earth caused them to seek His blessed Person and His abode, leading them on toward the heavenly home above from which He came and where He has returned. How blest a home!

Are we attracted to Christ by His walk? Do we follow the lowly and perfect path of the Son of God, noting from the inspired record how He walked? What lessons there are for us if we will study the path of Christ from the manger to the Cross, the only example for us to follow. It unerringly led downward, a path of humiliation that brought Him ultimately to "the death of the cross" (Phil. 2:5-8). We should be attracted to Him by His walk and seek to "follow His steps" (1 Pet. 2:21). It will attract us even more to His blessed Person.

3. *Some were attracted to Christ by His death:* "And I, if I be lifted up from the earth, will draw all unto Me...signifying what death He should die." With millions of others, we realize that we were first attracted to Him by His atoning and vicarious death. Christ points to His crucifixion by using the same expression spoken to Nicodemus in John 3:14-15. Crucified, He has become the great center of attraction, drawing to Himself multitudes from all peoples, nations, and countries, delivering them from the power of Satan, sin, death, and hell!

These words may even look further, when on the basis of His death and His future exaltation, "every knee should bow, of things in heaven, and things in earth, and things under the earth; and that every tongue should confess that Jesus Christ is Lord, to the glory of God the Father" (Phil. 2:10-11). Yet we must not assume that these words support the deadly heresy of a universal salvation that all men shall actually be saved. His salvation is "unto all" but only "upon all them that believe."

Is there any subject that touches the heart of a believer so deeply as the thoughts of His death? Shall we ever be able to comprehend the fullness of His love and grace that was perfectly displayed toward us by the cross? Not alone in the weekly remembrance of the Lord's Supper, but each moment of life our hearts can dwell on the wonder of His love.

"Death, death of stricken love, wrath's sea exploring!
Death, Life's mysterious death—deep meeting deep!
Death, whence Thy bursting heart fills ours outpouring
All, all in worship, Lord, low at Thy feet." (F. Allaben)

4. *Some were attracted to Christ by His burial:* Have you noticed that in the account of the Saviour's burial only two men and two women are mentioned as attendants to His funeral? They were Joseph of Arimathea and Nicodemus; and the two Marys (see Mt. 27:61). How remarkable that the men had been secret disciples to the time of His death, but when His precious body hung lifeless on the cross, they openly demanded Pilate to be given the custody of His body for burial, when all His professing disciples had fled! They are no longer secret disciples, for above all others Joseph and Nicodemus valued the blessed body of their Lord. Tenderly removing it from the Cross, they cleansed it for burial and wrapped it "in linen clothes with the spices" (Jn. 19:38-40). How the scripture was carefully fulfilled: "And He made His grave with the wicked, and with the rich in His death" (Isa. 53:9). This will be eternally remembered by God.

Yet it was an interrupted funeral, for "death could not keep its prey." What an attachment these two men and two women manifested to even the lifeless body of their blessed Lord and Saviour. What are our thoughts concerning this? Sacred and precious thoughts can be ours if we will dwell on the amazing fact of our Saviour's body being lifeless between His death and His resurrection—His spirit and soul in the unseen realm of the dead while His precious body lies in the tomb lifeless. Has there ever been such an historic event and tremendous fact of divine history embraced in this experience of the Lord of life, the Son of God, being in death? And it was all for our salvation!

5. *Some are attracted to Christ in glory:* The last Scripture reveals faithful Stephen being stoned to death by his persecutors; yet not even the violent circumstances surrounding his martyrdom could prevent him from "being full of the Holy Ghost" and "looking up steadfastly into heaven" to see "the glory of God, and Jesus standing on the right hand of God" (Acts 7:55). Even in death, His heart was attracted to Christ in glory! "I see the

heavens opened and the Son of Man standing on the right hand of God" was his triumphant cry. What a vision was his! The glorified Christ was seen waiting to receive him. "Lord Jesus, receive my spirit," he said. And again, "Lay not this sin to their charge," as he prayed for his enemies. What mattered the suffering and the cruelty heaped upon his body? The heavens were opening and his heart was completely occupied with Christ above in glory! Heaven was completely attracting him to the glorious Person of His risen, ascended and now glorified Lord.

What about us, beloved? Will Christ in glory be *our* attraction in death when that moment comes for us? Why not? One truth is certain, if we make Him our attraction during life then He certainly will be the same for us in death.

Should we not be completely attracted to Christ—by His birth, by His walk, by His death, by His burial; and at the journey's end be attracted to Christ in glory? Forever in eternal glory we shall be occupied with His blessed Person and attracted to Him forever! He will make heaven, heaven. Is He not worthy of this now? Yes, "The Person of Christ is the perfect object for the heart."

"O patient, spotless One! Our hearts in meekness train
To bear Thy yoke and learn of Thee that we may rest obtain.

Saviour! Thou art enough the mind and heart to fill;
Thy life, to calm the anxious soul, Thy love its fear dispel.

O fix our earnest gaze so wholly, Lord, on Thee,
That with Thy beauty occupied, we elsewhere none may see."
(Mrs. E. Helyer)

17

At Rest in Bethany

How dear to the heart of Christ was Bethany during His earthly life (Mt. 21:12-17; Lk. 10:38-42). He preferred Bethany to Jerusalem. The latter should have been His resting place. The Psalmist wrote, "For the Lord hath chosen Zion; He hath desired it for His habitation, This is My rest forever: here will I dwell; for I have desired it" (Ps. 132:13-14). But the Lord found no rest and satisfaction there. This is clearly seen by His act of indignation when He drove out "all them that sold and bought in the temple, and overthrew the tables of the money-changers" (Mt. 21:12). He would not lodge in Jerusalem: "He left them and went out of the city into Bethany and lodged there" (Mt. 21:17). It was an act of complete abandonment, even though Jerusalem was the center of the divine testimony in Israel What a tragedy! But why was Bethany His preference?

1. *Bethany was the place of His satisfaction and rest:* Although there is some difference of opinion about what Bethany means, it has been suggested to mean "the house of figs." Jerusalem had become a barren fig tree, producing "nothing but leaves" and was cursed (Mt. 21:18-19). Bethany was the place of fruit for the Lord, a place of rest and satisfaction for Him. Devoted saints opened their hearts and home to welcome their heavenly Guest there. There, with joy, He could rest (read Zeph. 3:17).

It is still the long night of His rejection, and in the midst of chaotic conditions in the world and professing Christendom, where can the Lord find satisfaction and rest? Wherever a company of devoted saints, though small, will give Him the place of centrality, there He will lodge "in the midst" (Mt. 18:20). Is this true of your assembly? Are our hearts real Bethanys for Him? Are we loyal to Him and faithful to His Word?

2. *Bethany was the place of His recognition and reception:* The "certain village" in Luke 10:38 was Bethany, we know; where Martha "received Him into her house." What a contrast to Jerusalem and the nation, over which He wept! (Lk. 19:41). Martha's heart and home welcomed the Saviour. Recognized and received, He was their honored guest. There He found genuine love and hospitality during His earthly years of trial and suffering. An eternal bond of fellowship began for Martha, Mary, and Lazarus when they received Him.

Others since then have been added to this fellowship. The three thousand souls who were converted at Pentecost, who "gladly received his word" (Acts 2:41)—each one became another Bethany for Him. Lydia and her household too "attended unto the things which were spoken of Paul" (Acts 16:14-15) and her heart and home became another Bethany for Him. Multitudes since have also received Him; you and I receive Him and become another Bethany for Him to enjoy (Jn. 1:12). Are we giving Him the true meaning of Bethany? Do we acknowledge His Lordship and authority? What a privilege and what a responsibility! Does He enjoy lodging with us?

3. *Bethany was the place of deep spiritual lessons* (Lk. 10:39-42): "That only is important which is eternal" has well been said. At Bethany, Mary found this to be true. Sitting "at Jesus' feet," she heard His words, drinking in the revelation of His glorious Person and His teaching of eternal truth. What lessons! Martha, unfortunately, had to learn that *knowing* the Lord must come before *serving* the Lord. Mary found "that good part" at Bethany, which the Saviour said "shall not be taken away from her." Are we proving this? Is your heart and mine this kind of a Bethany? Or are we like Martha: "anxious and troubled about many things"? How we need to get low like Mary and sit "at the feet of Jesus." Do we know the meaning of Bethany *to Him*?

"Low at Thy feet, Lord Jesus; this is the place for me;
Here I have learned deep lessons—truth that has set me free."

18
Jesus On the Journey

The "Emmaus" road (Lk. 24:15) stretches out before us. What the days ahead may hold for us is unknown for the greater part. We *do* know the Lord may come today! There are some spiritual lessons for us to learn from the journey of the two disciples long ago as they walked from Jerusalem to Emmaus in companionship with the Lord Jesus:

1. *The commencement of the journey:* For the two disciples, it began with the dark shadows of Calvary behind them, producing disappointment, despair, and doubt. Their hopes were shattered, their hearts were sad, and before them a seemingly forlorn future. Or so they thought, as they traveled the seven miles from the City of the Great King.

Outwardly, the background for us today is a dark one also. We live in a "dark place" while in this world (2 Pet. 1:19). Its ecclesiastical darkness is graphically described by Peter in his second epistle, chapter 2. Its infidel darkness is described in the third chapter of his epistle, atheism and agnosticism being rampant. In addition to this, we have the dark experiences of personal trials; they may be physical, moral or spiritual, all tending to make the heart sad. Nevertheless, if such is the case, we are not alone! We too can say, "Jesus Himself drew near and went with them."

2. *The compensation of the journey:* His blessed companionship stirred their hearts! Only He was able to explain their disappointments and cause them to see that "all things work together for good." From the riches of Holy Scripture, He was able to

79

open their minds to know that Christ must suffer before entering His glory (Lk. 24:25-27). Then He opened their eyes to behold that it was He Himself who was with them as they sat and broke bread together. They saw His pierced hands (Lk. 24:30-31). It was enough!

Beloved, whatever may be the condition, without or within, as we continue our pilgrimage, the presence of our Lord with us every moment is sure. Let Him open the Scriptures to our hearts through the year concerning Himself and open our minds with divine illumination revealing His glory. Permit Him to open our eyes also to see His loveliness as He abides with us through the year, day by day! We also are journeying, as He did, from sufferings to glory!

3. *The consummation of the journey:* It did not end at Emmaus. There was a twofold result for the two disciples and also for us. "They knew Him" (Lk. 20:31). A greater knowledge of His Person was theirs. May it be ours also (Phil. 3:10). Their doubts, discouragement, and despair vanished even as "He vanished out of their sight." Their lagging feet became lighter! Their heavy hearts became brighter! Their trembling lips became stronger! With His praises filling their souls, they hurried back to Jerusalem. Let us allow the Lord to lift our feet, fill our hearts, and empower our lips to give forth His praise!

Next, back in Jerusalem, the divine center from which they had sadly strayed, they returned with joy to a blessed reunion with the others. Better still was to discover that "Jesus Himself stood in the midst of them" (Lk. 24:36). What a climax to their journey on the Emmaus road—it could not be better! Around Him with His own! Beloved, the years ahead hold the same possibility for us, to be "caught up together...in the clouds, to meet the Lord in the air, and so shall we ever be with the Lord" (1 Thess. 4:17). What a blessed consummation to our journey that will be! What can we say but "Even so, come, Lord Jesus!"

19
The Magnitude of Divine Forgiveness

Have you considered the greatness of the Saviour's prayer from the Cross, addressed to His Father: "Father, forgive them for they know not what they do" (Lk. 23:34)? Though the objects of such intercession were ignorant of the Person crucified, yet His great heart of love prayed for them. Whom did He mean by "them"? Was the Son of God praying an unanswerable prayer? How could He? Yet ask yourself, For whom did He pray?

Did He pray for Judas? He had tenderly washed the traitor's feet (Jn. 13), knowing the evil design that was in his heart. He had given him the sop, the morsel of honor. When our Lord received the betrayal kiss, did He not lovingly plead, "Friend, wherefore art thou come?" (Mt. 26:50). It was perhaps the last pleading of love, for Judas probably did not witness the crucifixion if the record of Matthew 27:3-10 is in sequence. Can we doubt that if he had repented and cast himself at the foot of the Saviour's cross he would have found forgiveness? That precious blood flowing there could make the vilest clean. Yet he refused to repent and by a suicidal death entered into the darkness of eternity. Remorse filled his soul at the end, but he never received the forgiveness Christ offered. How many today are just like Judas in turning away from the offer of divine forgiveness!

Did He pray for Caiaphas and the rulers? What unsurpassing love He showed for His foes. Those bloodthirsty, ecclesiastical leaders had persecuted, despised, abused, and hounded Him all the days of His ministry. Now they were watching Him in wicked glee as He suffered on the cursed tree. Caiaphas had reached the pinnacle of his prophetic ministry as he saw the Son of God there (see Jn. 11:47-52). What success seemed to be his. Priests and scribes were a most contemptible lot, deserving of divine wrath! Yet from the lips of the holy Sufferer fell no word of bitterness, anger or curse. Just the quiet but sincere prayer: "Father, forgive them." In exchange for their blasphemies, brutality, and hatred, He prayed for their forgiveness. Has greater love ever been shown? Is it not probable that from among them some are referred to in Acts 6:7, where we read, "a great company of the priests were obedient to the faith." Did it not answer His prayer? Yes, He prayed for His bitterest enemies.

Did He pray for the rabble mob? They had united their voices to demand His death. Spurred on by their ungodly leaders, they chose a murderer, saying of Christ, "Away with Him!...Release unto us Barabbas" (Lk. 23:18). "Crucify Him," they cried (Jn. 19:15). Before His cross they gathered, deriding and saying, "If Thou be the Son of God, come down from the cross" (Mt. 27:40). As they passed by, the jeering mob hurled words of derision and hatred. How could they do so in view of all He had done for them? Yet what did He say? "Father, forgive them." How unworthy they were of His forgiveness, yet before we would condemn them, let us ask, "Am I worthy of it?" May we not be assured that on the day of Pentecost and subsequent days, many of these men were among the early believers of the Church, an answer to that magnanimous prayer? Certainly we must say that His prayer was not unanswerable. (Read Acts 2:35-42.) He prayed for that rabble crowd.

Did He pray for the Roman authorities? For Pilate, the governor? Was it possible for him to be forgiven? Why not? Yet we doubt that he ever was. The soldiers who crowned Him with thorns— who mocked Him, who spit upon Him, who smote Him on the head and spiked Him to the tree? Those who pierced His blessed side—could they be forgiven? Was not the centurion in charge of the execution a probable believer and included in His prayer? The soldiers who gambled for His seamless robe—could they be forgiven? All were pagan Romans hardened to the cruelties of war and Roman executions, yet how they must have marvelled to hear the holy Sufferer pray: "Father, forgive them!"

They were accustomed to hear oaths and curses from their victims but from His lips they heard the prayer for their forgiveness! They had no Messianic hopes; no promise of redemption was contained in their pagan philosophy, yet did not the centurion say, "Certainly, this Man was a righteous man," as He saw the Saviour die (Lk. 23:47). "Truly this Man was the Son of God" (Mk. 15:39). The magnitude of His forgiveness embraced His executioners and the Roman officials at His death. What mystery of love is this!

Did He pray for the two malefactors? The thieves also, which were crucified with Him, cast their derision on the Saviour" (Mt. 27:44). They were close enough to hear that prayer. Were they not included, though rightfuly paying for their criminal deeds, the judicial penalty deserved? One hardened his heart forever, railing on the Saviour, demanding deliverance for himself in selfishness. Suddenly, the work of conscience was manifested by his fellow companion in crime, as he rebuked his fellow: "Dost not thou fear God, seeing thou art in the same condemnation? And we indeed justly; for we receive the due reward of our deeds" (Lk. 23:40-41). His guilt he confesses; but in repentance and surrender he turns to the Saviour, saying, "But this Man hath done nothing amiss." Here is another confession of the Lord's sinless humanity. To the Lord, he says, "Lord, remember me when Thou comest into Thy kingdom." Here now is a confession of His Deity! Was he saved? Listen to the words of Jesus in Matthew 10:32, "Whosoever...shall confess Me before men, him will I confess also before My Father which is in heaven." Was he forgiven? Was the Saviour's prayer answered? Hear the words of divine assurance to the thief: "Verily I say unto thee, Today shalt thou be with Me in paradise" (Lk. 23:43). He requested a place in the kingdom; yet Jesus says he needs not wait for that day. "Today [not when the day of His glory and power comes] shalt thou be with Me [better than being remembered] in paradise [better than an earthly kingdom]."

The Saviour expired before the death of the penitent thief; so that when the spirit of the thief departed his body, he found the Saviour was waiting for him in paradise. What a joyful meeting that must have been! "With Me," the Lord had said. Though on the cross the thief had no hope, his life fast ebbing away, yet in repentance and faith he found the Lord's prayer answered—he was forgiven, and forever "with Christ which is far better." Yes, the Saviour's prayer was answered!

Did He pray for you and me? Far beyond the horizon of the crucifixion scene, the Saviour saw the whole world of humanity before Him. He saw you and He saw me! We all, under sin's blindness and Satan's domination, united our voices in rejection of the Son of God. The world is still saying, "Away with Him! Crucify Him!" Yes, your sins and my sins placed the Saviour on that cross. Our sins were borne by Him there. Yet before the great heart of the Son of God was the longing for a world of sinners to be redeemed. He still is heard saying that "repentance and remission of sins should be preached in His Name among all nations" (Lk. 24:47). Is it a universal redemption? Is it a universal propitiation? According to 1 John 2:2, it is! His great prayer embraces all: "Father, forgive them"!

Dare any person limit the magnitude of divine forgiveness? What a travesty to the heart of the Son of God it would be to do so! Does it exclude any human being? God forgive such a thought, though all do not come to repentance and live; they can if they will! For all the Saviour prays: "Father, forgive them!" My friend, has He forgiven you? Have you received His gift of salvation? If not, receive His forgiveness right now.

> *"Forgive them, O forgive," He cried;*
> *Then bowed His sacred head;*
> *O Lamb of God, my Sacrifice,*
> *For me Thy blood was shed.*
>
> *His voice I hear, His love I know;*
> *I worship at His feet;*
> *And kneeling there, at Calvary's cross,*
> *Redemption is complete.*
>
> *Crucified! Crucified!*
> *And nailed upon a tree;*
> *With pierced hands and feet and side,*
> *For you, for me!*   (C. Austin Miles)

20
The Seven Consolations of Christ

In John 14:1-27, beginning with the words, "Let not your heart be troubled," and ending with the words, "Let not your heart be troubled, neither let it be afraid," the Saviour gives seven consolations for "His own" left in the world. They are words of great comfort for us until He comes to take us home.

Consolation One: Our reunion with Him in the Father's home above (vv. 1-3). He reveals six facts about the home. 1. *Its reality* (vv. 1-2). This is based upon our faith in God, in Christ, and in His Word. 2. *Its locality* (v. 2). It is a definite "place" in distance far beyond our comprehension, but where the Father dwells, where the Son reigns with His holy angels, and where loved ones are now "with Christ." 3. *Its felicity* (v. 1). No troubles there! "Let not your heart be troubled," He said. It is a home of rest (Heb. 4:9); joy (Ps. 16:11); love (1 Cor. 13:13); fellowship (Rev. 21:3; 22:3-5). 4. *Its immensity* (v. 2). There are many mansions. Multitudes will be there! (Rev. 5:11; 7:9). The home will be filled (Lk. 14:23; Isa. 53:11). (5) *Its permanency* (v. 2). The Greek word for "mansions" describes its abiding character. This is our permanent Home! (Heb. 11:10; 13:14). (6) *Its imminency* (v. 3). "I am coming again," He promised. He is coming personally (1 Thess. 4:16); suddenly (1 Cor. 15:52); and quickly (Rev. 22:7,12,20). Perhaps today! Blessed consolation!

Consolation Two: We know the way to the Father's home (vv. 4-11). *The way is a Person,* One whom we have trusted. *The way is sufficient.* Why? Because He is also the Truth, the full and perfect revelation of God His Father (Heb. 1:3; Col. 1:19) and He is the

Life, the personal embodiment of what God is (1 Jn. 5:12). *The way is exclusive.* This is of great significance because He is the only way—not one of many ways (Jn. 10:9; Acts 4:12; 1 Cor. 3:11; 1 Tim. 2:5). To come to the Father is fully revealed in and by the Son. We must understand that when we come to the Son we come to the Father. Then with confidence we can say, We know the way. Blessed consolation!

Consolation Three: Though now in heaven, our glorified Lord still works on earth (vv. 12-14). His chosen vessel is the believer (v. 12). The character of the works through such willing servants are similar to His own (v. 12). His early disciples did them (Acts. 3:6-8; 9:40; 14:10; 16:18; 20:12). Also, greater works will His own do, miracles of a spiritual kind. (Peter, Acts 2:41; Philip, Acts 8:5-12; Paul, on all his missionary travels). Why greater works? "Because I go to My Father" (see Jn. 7:37-39; Jn. 16:7). The exaltation of Christ and the descent of the Spirit has produced these "greater works." How is the work done (vv. 13-14)? Through communication between Christ and the believers by prayer to the Father, the believer communicates with Him, but the Lord Himself is the real worker. We are only His instruments. He continues to work through us: "Without Me," He reminded us, "ye can do nothing" (Jn. 15:5).

Consolation Four: The promise of another Comforter (vv. 15-17). This Paraclete is personal and divine, One who the Lord says is like Himself. He is equal with the Father and the Son, though He is distinct from both. The condition of enjoying Him is simply love for the Lord and our obedience to His Word (v. 15). Then we discover two blessed facts. First, there is His *permanent* presence—"with you forever" (v. 16). And there is His *indwelling* presence—"in you." The Spirit of truth is His name, and He is with us to reveal all truth. We know Him, but the world knows Him not. Can we ever lose Him? Never! Precious Saviour and blessed consolation!

Consolation Five: The return of the glorified Christ (vv. 18-24). This is a spiritual coming, not His final coming; not after the resurrection of the dead in Christ, but a return in the Person of the Holy Spirit. It is personal, for He promises, "I will come to you" (v. 18). Note also verses 21 and 23. During our Lord's sojourn on earth, the Spirit was personally present with Him. So after His departure, Christ is personally present with us by the Spirit. By faith "Ye see me!" (Heb. 2:9). We participate in His risen life (v. 19). We apprehend His greatness, His oneness with the Father; our oneness with Him; and His oneness with us (v. 20). He reveals Himself and His Father (vv. 21, 23). Are we enjoying this? It is a blessed consolation!

Consolation Six: The mission of the Holy Spirit (vv. 25-26). The Holy Spirit should be held in highest esteem. He is the saints' Comforter. He is the Father's commissioned representative, sent by the Father. He is the believer's Teacher: "He shall teach you all things." He is the Christian's Remembrancer.: He will "bring all things to your remembrance." He is the Saviour's expositor: "...in whatsoever I have said unto you." Concerning more of His work, read John 15:26; 16:7-13. Without His ministry, Christ would never be revealed nor understood. The Spirit possesses the twofold approval and authority of the Father and the Son. We can depend on Him!

Consolation Seven: The Saviour's legacy of peace for all circumstances (v. 27). It is the peace of contentment in all our circumstances. This peace the world can never learn, nor give us. Unrest and discontentment prevail among men today. Only one Man has appeared on earth who never needed to search for peace! From the beginning of His life right to the end, He possessed it. He was never rebellious, never ruffled, never fretting over His external circumstances or the privations which He endured. The reproaches He encountered, the sufferings He bore, and even the death He died, never disturbed His peace. In the midst of it all, He had "perfect peace" (Isa. 26:3). This same peace He has bequeathed to all of His own. He gives it generously, sincerely, and permanently. This legacy the Saviour has given us to sustain us in the midst of all our trials. It is not merely a peace that He can impart but a peace which is found in Him—"My peace." Is it ours today? Blessed consolation!

What is the purpose of these seven consolations? "Let not your heart be troubled, neither let it be afraid." Our blessed Lord unfolds these great consolations from His own loving heart to the hearts of His followers, to strengthen them in view of His departure out of this world to the Father and to sustain His own until He comes back. Is there trouble? Is there sadness of heart? Is there discouragement? Whatever our lot, His consolations of love will see us through to the end. May we appreciate them today!

"Great legacy He left His own,
'Twas left to them, to them alone—
The peace which He Himself had known.

This peace would keep us every day
'Midst all the world's distracted fray;
We may possess it now, alway.

No effort brings it to our door:
Nor need we for its wealth implore;
'Tis ours; exhaustless in its store.

How comes it? Well, 'My peace I give,'
'Tis ours as we His Word believe;
It keeps—as we its wealth receive."

Let us love Him; let us rejoice that He is with the Father and enjoy His consolations until He returns. He is at Home with His Father and we shall be there very soon!

21
The Blessings of His Absence

The Saviour said, "Ye have heard how I said unto you, I go away, and come again unto you. If you loved Me, you would rejoice, because I said, I go unto the Father: for My Father is greater than I" (Jn. 14:28). Have we fully appreciated the meaning of His words when He said, "Nevertheless, I tell you the truth; It is expedient for you that I go away: for if I go not away, the Comforter will not come unto you; but if I depart, I will send Him unto you" (Jn. 16:7)? The announcement of His departure to the Father in preceding chapters had produced great sorrow of heart to the disciples. His coming absence troubled them greatly and now He tells them it would be more profitable for them to be without His bodily presence on the earth. Do we have greater blessings because of this today?

His presence is nearer: In His incarnate flesh, He was confined to one location at a time when on earth. Now, He is beyond the boundaries of time and sense, filling all things above and accessible by faith and prayer to all of His own (Eph. 1:22-23). We all have access into His immediate presence today, no matter where on earth we live. Furthermore, His presence with us is also assured, for He has said, "Lo, I am with you alway, even unto the end of the [ages]" (Mt. 28:20). Many promises has He given us (such as Mt. 18:20; Phil. 4:5; Heb. 13:5-6, etc.). Is it not true today that we can know the preciousness in our daily walk of those words recorded in Luke 24:15, that "Jesus Himself drew near, and went with them"? Though absent from earth, there is not a child of God in the whole world out of His reach; to every one of His own His presence is nearer.

His Godhead is clearer: There were occasions when the hearts and minds of His disciples who walked with the Lord could not grasp His great Godhead as He walked and lived with them each day. Occasional glimpses of His glorious deity were visible to their eyes, but often the question was raised, "What manner of *Man* is this?" (Mk. 4:41). Yet when His resurrection and exaltation in heaven was established, beyond all controversy His glorious deity was more fully comprehended by His disciples than if He had stayed on earth. All the subsequent ministry and writings of His apostles and disciples indicate that to them His Godhead was better understood. Then He was "declared to be the Son of God with power, according to the Spirit of holiness, by the resurrection from the dead" (Rom. 1:4). When Christ took His place "on the right hand of the Majesty on high" then they knew with absolute assurance that He was "higher than the angels" (Heb. 1:3-5). For them, and for us today His Godhead is clearer.

His salvation is surer: How precious to know the strong and eternal assurance we have concerning His perfect redemption that is ours, all because He is absent from earth and present in heaven! The evidence is perfect, that His redemption work is complete. Listen to the words of Hebrews 10:12, 14, "But this Man, after He had offered one sacrifice for sins forever sat down on the right hand of God...For by one offering He hath perfected forever them that are sanctified." Again, "He entered once into the holy place, having obtained eternal redemption for us" (Heb. 9:12). Yes, because He is there in heaven, His great salvation is surer.

His heaven is dearer: There would be no attraction to the Father's home above if Christ had stayed on earth among men; but by His presence above He is the greatest attraction there to the hearts of His own. "And if I go and prepare a place for you, I will come again and receive you unto Myself, that where I am, there ye may be also" (Jn. 14:3. See also 1 Thess. 4:13-18; 1 Jn. 3:2; Rev. 5:6-14). All the outward display of heaven's glory cannot compare with the preciousness of His blessed Person. Beloved Samuel Rutherford has well written his conviction of this, saying, "I would be in heaven, if I had no other reason but to see that golden Ark, and God inhabiting a body such as we sinners have, that I might adore Him for evermore." Is not this our conviction, too? We have loved ones in His presence above waiting for the glad reunion of saints at His coming. Yet without Him being there, it never could be heaven for them or for us. Because He is not here, but there, our departed saints are enjoying Him! To them heaven is dearer, and for us who wait the glad day when we too shall be taken Home, it is also blessedly true that heaven is nearer since He took our hearts captive there.

His Church is richer: His departure has not robbed us at all, but has made us richer on the earth because of the indwelling presence and the power of His Holy Spirit. Did He not say, "For if I go not away, the Comforter will not come unto you; but if I depart, I will send Him unto you" (Jn. 16:7). Has He not kept this promise? Has He not sent an equally divine Person who is not limited to a human body? He is not only with us but in us! The church is richer because of the coming of the Holy Spirit to the earth, coming at Pentecost and continuing with the Church until the blessed rapture of the saints.

With the redemption work *now* fully completed by Christ, the presence *now* of the Holy Spirit on the earth, the Lord Jesus Christ can *now* in the most blessed and intimate manner bring our hearts into all the eternal values that flow from Christ and His work. It is His delight to reveal to us God the Father's estimation of His Son who is in heaven. This never could be done until His absence from earth, and His presence in heaven. It was a necessary change of ministry, changing it from the visible to the invisible, from the earthly to the heavenly, from the external to the internal, and from the occasional to the perpetual. For all of this has the Holy Spirit been given, to bring to the hearts of His own what we have in that blessed Man in the glory.

Properly has the apostle Paul written, "Blessed be the God and Father of our Lord Jesus Christ, who hath blessed us with all spiritual blessings in heavenly places in Christ" (Eph. 1:3). All those unsearchable riches in Christ that are now ours should be enjoyed by us on the earth, which never could be if that blessed Man was not absent on earth and present in heaven above.

"He shall glorify Me: for He shall receive of Mine, and shall show it unto you. All things that the Father hath are Mine: therefore said I, that He shall take of Mine, and shall show it unto you," said the Lord Jesus (Jn. 16:14-15). The riches of His Church are not measured by earthly standards. They are all in that Man in the glory at the right hand of God. But the Revealer of all those riches in Him is the Holy Spirit of God.

No doubt Eliezer, the servant of Abraham, delighted in telling Rebecca, the espoused wife of Isaac, of his master and his riches as they traveled the long desert journey toward the land of Canaan. Does the Holy Spirit have the present delight and opportunity to speak to our hearts of our riches in that blessed One in heaven? As we travel through this wilderness, are we enjoying our riches in the exalted Lord? God grant that we do and shall more and more!

> *"This world is a wilderness wide,*
> *I have nothing to seek or to choose;*
> *I've no thought in the waste to abide;*
> *I've naught to regret or to lose.*
>
> *The path where my Saviour is gone,*
> *Has led up to His Father and God;*
> *To the place where He's now on the throne,*
> *His strength shall be mine on the road"* (J. N. Darby)

22
Unfinished Business

One great proof of our Lord's resurrection is the work per-
formed by Him on the first resurrection day. It was a ministry
that has continued down to this day, and will continue to the
end of the Christian age. "Smite the Shepherd, and the sheep
shall be scattered" was predicted by Zechariah the prophet
(Zech 13:7). These words were fulfilled (Mt. 26:3l; Mk. 14:50),
but as soon as our Lord was risen from the dead, He immediate-
ly sought those scattered sheep. He worked that first resurrection day to gather His disciples together; and at the end of the
day, they were once more around their blessed Shepherd. What
He accomplished that day, He has been doing ever since!

A sorrowing heart is the first object of His search. To Mary
Magdalene, sorrowing for Him above all others in her devotion,
He first revealed Himself (Jn. 20:11-18). "They have taken away
my Lord, and I know not where they have laid Him," was her
grief-stricken cry. The whole world was black for her without
Him. Not even a vision of celestial angels could solace her, for
she wanted Him and Him alone! Her desire and devotion
exceeded her physical strength as she said, "Tell me where thou
hast laid Him, and I will take Him away."

So to the sorrowing heart of Mary, the Lord first ministered
His resurrection grace, turning her sorrow into joy, her tears into
laughter, and her mourning into gladness. He calls His own by
name and Jesus said to her, "Mary!" Then she knew Him and
her sorrow vanished. He commissioned her to renewed service,
saying, "Go to My brethren and say unto them, I ascend unto

My Father, and your Father, and to My God and your God."

Sorrowing hearts! The world is filled with them; but here is One, the risen Lord, who has ministered through the centuries to countless multitudes, bringing His great grace and pardon in redemption power. Sorrow, the result of sin, covers the earth, but praise God for the power of the Son of God to bring the joy of forgiveness. He is ready to minister this right now to every heart sorrowing for sin, for He continues to say, "Behold, I stand at the door, and knock: if any man hear My voice, and open the door, I will come in to him, and will sup with him, and he with Me" (Rev. 3:20). To the sorrowing saints, who but the risen Lord can minister the comfort so greatly needed in the midst of their trials? Thank God, He lives for us!

A soiled conscience is the next object of His ministry on that first day of resurrection. The angel had said, "Tell His disciples and Peter..." (Mk. 16:7). It was a special message for Peter. Why? Peter had a very soiled conscience, for fellowship with his Lord had been broken through his denial of the Saviour. Bitter tears of remorse had flowed from the broken heart of the disciple at the realization of his terrible deed. Yet who can forgive like Christ? The great, tender heart of the Son of God planned a reconciliation. When did it happen and where? We shall never know, unless Peter tells us some day. But there was a meeting between Peter and his Lord alone, for we know it took place. "The Lord is risen indeed, and hath appeared to Simon!" (Lk. 24:34). Blessed reconciliation! Peter was restored and his soiled conscience cleansed. Hallelujah! What a Saviour!

Have you a soiled conscience, whether you are a saint or a sinner? A secret meeting with the risen Lord will settle the whole thing for you. "If we confess our sins, He is faithful and just to forgive us our sins, and to cleanse us from all unrighteousness" (1 Jn. 1:9). Who but our risen Lord can deal with a guilty conscience in the power of His own blood? "The blood of Jesus Christ His Son cleanseth us from all sin" (1 Jn. 1:7). So today, multitudes of soiled consciences on earth can come under the efficacy of the precious blood of Christ: "How much more shall the blood of Christ...purge your conscience" (Heb. 9:14).

The straying feet of two disciples traveling to Emmaus are the object of the Lord's tender care that same day of resurrection (Lk. 24:13-35). They were walking the Emmaus road of doubt, despair, discouragement, and disillusionment. As they dragged their weary hearts and feet back to their home, they believed that all was finished now. Christ their Master had died! He was not to be found, not even His body could be located. Where He was, they did not know, and counted everything now finished for them; their hopes had been all in Him. Even these must be brought back to the great Shepherd and so "Jesus Himself drew near and went with them" (Lk. 24:15). The living Saviour! What a change He brings as He speaks to these straying ones: straying from Jerusalem. Now, with new joy, new strength, and a new message, they hasten to tell the others: "He is risen!"

Yes, He still walks the Emmaus road of doubt and despair with His people! "I will never leave thee nor forsake thee," is His promise (Heb. 13:5-6). He is living today; and with every believer He walks the daily path of life. If you are straying from Him, let Him minister to your heart today and bring you back into fellowship with Himself. If you are a straying sinner, listen to His tender love pleading to your soul, "Come unto Me, all ye that labor and are heavy laden, and I will give you rest" (Mt. 11:28). He is still the Shepherd, seeking lost ones and straying sheep, blessed be His Name!

The final result of that day's ministry is recorded in John 20:19-23 and in Luke 24:36-48. As the disciples are gathered together in Jerusalem with the doors shut for fear of the Jews, "Then the same day at evening, being the first day of the week...came Jesus and stood in the midst, and saith unto them, Peace be unto you." The risen Lord was in the midst of His sheep and those who had been scattered were again around their beloved Shepherd! There was Peter; and Mary Magdalene; and the two straying ones from Emmaus, with the others of the disciples with them. Hallelujah! They were around Him once more. No wonder it is written, "Then were the disciples glad when they saw the Lord." Yes, they were glad to see Him alive. Yes, He was glad to have them back around Himself!

This is what He desires every resurrection day; every Lord's Day; every first day of the week—His own around Himself in worship, love, and praise. Men and women, who once possessed sorrowing hearts, soiled consciences, and straying feet, brought back by matchless grace from the paths of sin and sorrow, to gather them in love and gratitude around the great Shepherd. What a picture! Yet, it is only a miniature of the great meeting in heaven when He will gather His saints *forever* around Himself, taking them *forever* away from the sorrows of life, the sins of earth and the wandering path of this world, where they shall never again grieve, nor sin, nor wander!

Still today, the risen Lord desires to reach the sorrowful hearts, the soiled consciences, and the straying feet of men and women. Are we helping Him to fulfill this ministry? "Then Jesus said unto them again, Peace be unto you; as My Father hath sent Me, even so send I you" (Jn. 20:21). Let us look around us and see them, as we were once, sorrowing in sin, soiled in conscience, and straying from Him. And by His grace may we minister in the power of His resurrection to bring them to Himself. His great resurrection work—begun on the first resurrection day—must go on until He comes.

23
Perfections of the Lamb

Out from the numerous and glorious names given to Christ in the Word of God, the special one purposely designated for prominence in the book of Revelation is "the Lamb." It is repeated twenty-eight times in all, being expressed in the diminutive, meaning literally "the little lamb." Why should this name be predominant in the book of judgment and glory? Two reasons may be profitably suggested.

First, God's beloved Son was led "as a lamb to the slaughter" (Isa. 53:7) and it is written, "His visage was so marred more than any man, and His form more than the sons of men" (Isa. 52:13). This was allowed to do the will of God for our redemption. Thus He descended into incomprehensible sufferings and humiliation for our sins (Isa. 53:5-6). For this reason, God declares that His holy Servant "shall be exalted and lifted up and be high very much, or exceedingly" (Isa. 52:13, lit. Heb. Trans.). An ancient Rabbinic Midrash says, "He shall be exalted above Abraham; He shall be lifted up above Moses, and be higher than the ministering angels." Therefore, we should not wonder that God delights to take that name of deepest humiliation and crown it with the highest exaltation in the end book of the Bible.

Secondly, the name of the "Lamb" is also the most precious of all titles to His blood-bought church, the Bride, for two reasons. First, it is to her His sacrificial name, telling the story of an eternal redemption that He paid to purchase her for Himself (Rev. 5:8-11). Second, it is also to her His bridal name, unfolding His eternal affection that will be her delight (Rev. 19:6-9). Surely no other body of saints in eternity will appreciate the name of the Lamb like those who compose the Bride of the Lamb. This is indicated in the description of her heavenly glory as John saw the city of New Jerusalem (Rev 21:9-22:5). This precious name of the Lamb is mentioned seven times, indicating Him to be the center of all, and describing the perfections of the Lamb with eternal pre-eminence and to the delight of her heart.

The perfections of His love: "I will show thee the bride, the Lamb's wife" (Rev. 21:9). She is the fruit of His affection, His redemption, His ministration, and His glorification (see Eph. 5:25-27). She is the "pearl of great price" for which He "went and sold all that He had, and bought it" (Mt. 13:46). Possessing "the glory of God" (Rev. 21:10-11), she will be the satisfying object for His eternal love, perfectly suitable for His great heart. The perfection of His love will thus be realized, as the heavenly saints shall be for Him and to Him a perfect and eternal Bride! He who has loved us with infinite perfection will then have for Himself a perfect Bride forever. He then will rejoice in the fruit of His perfect love. We shall sing through endless ages our song of that perfect love: "Unto Him that loveth us and hath [loosed] us from our sins in His own blood, and hath made us kings and priests unto God and his Father; to Him be glory and dominion forever and ever. Amen" (Rev. 1:5-6).

The perfection of His work: "And the wall of the city had twelve foundations, and in them the names of the twelve apostles of the Lamb" (Rev. 21:14). The detailed description of the glorious city of gold, with its great capacity, perfect symmetry, brilliant walls of jasper, twelve pearly gates, the street of gold and the garnished foundations studded with precious jewels, all reflect the infinite wisdom and perfect work of the Lamb as the architect and builder (Rev. 21:11-21). The devoted labors of the twelve apostles are graciously and eternally acknowledged by Him (Rev. 21:14; 1 Cor. 3:11; Eph. 2:19-22), but it is the Lamb Himself who originated, inaugurated, and will complete the infinite work of grace to possess His Bride (Mt. 16:16-18). The perfect workmanship of the city is likened to "pure gold like to clear glass." An object is presented, the splendor of which far outshines the sublimest creation of human dreams.

Yet, what is a city without inhabitants? The perfection of the New Jerusalem is not complete without the presence of His sanctified and glorified saints dwelling there. They also are His workmanship (Eph. 2:10), and are necessary to complete what the angel calls "the Bride, the Lamb's wife" as she appears in her final form and character. They have been begotten by His Spirit, formed and fashioned into living stones from the darkness of sin and the quarry of a fallen world (1 Pet. 2:5), and transfigured from glory to glory (2 Cor. 3:18) until they reach eternal perfection above. To briefly summarize the completeness of the Lamb's work, we quote the concise words of another: "He who makes, prepares and places them, makes, prepares, and places their sublime habitation" (J. A. Seiss).

The perfection of His holiness: "And I saw no temple therein: for the Lord God Almighty and the Lamb are the temple of it" (Rev. 21:22). Two words are used in the Greek New Testament for "temple": *hieron* means the whole temple area with all its buildings; *naos* implies the inner sanctuary of the holy place and the holiest of all. This latter word is used in our text, indicating to the apostle John in the vision that there was no material sanctuary to be seen in the city. God Himself and the Lamb will be the temple there, the Shekinah glory encompassing the saints and all the city alike, which will enable the glorious worshippers to hold direct communion with God and the Lamb. "As consecrated high priests, they will then have come into the holiest of all, into the very cloud of God's overshadowing glory, which is at once their covering, their temple, their God. And when the saints in immortal glory dwell within the enclosing light of the unveiled presence of God and the Lamb, as His Bride and Wife, what more need have they of temple, or outward ceremonial, to commune with deity, or to have fellowship with the Father and the Son? Their worship is immediate and direct" (J. A. Seiss). Praise the Lord! We shall enjoy forever the perfection of God's holiness and presence.

The perfection of His illumination: "And the city had no need of the sun, neither of the moon, to shine in it: for the glory of God did lighten it, and the Lamb is the light thereof" (Rev. 21:23). "The moon shall be confounded and the sun ashamed," writes the prophet (Isa. 24:23), because of the outshining glory that will be in the New Jerusalem, leaving them no more need to shine in it, since the glory of God lights it and the Lamb is the light thereof. The glory of God's brightness will envelope, permeate, and radiate through the city, causing its brilliant rays to shine over all the earth, through the reaches of outer space, making the heavenly planet seem to distant worlds a brilliant illuminary whose brightness will never fail or wane! Greater still, to the hearts of the inhabitants of the city, will be the spiritual light that will illuminate the understanding of the soul with the eternal and spiritual glories of God and the Lamb through never-ending ages. "And this is life eternal, that they might know Thee, the only true God, and Jesus Christ, whom Thou hast sent," stated God's Son in John 17:3. The eternal ages for the inhabitants of that city will be spent going on, and on, and on, learning more and more of the glories of God and His beloved Son. What a blessed way to spend eternity!

The perfection of His protection: "And there shall in no wise enter into it anything that defileth, neither whatsoever worketh abomination, or maketh a lie: but they which are written in the Lamb's book of life" (Rev. 21:27). This incorruptible inheritance will never be defiled, for out of the myriads of human souls through all human history, no one can ever set foot on its golden street who is not enrolled in the book of life of the Lamb. He is the perfect guardian of the city and its eternal purity. Sinners may come there, yes; for sinners it was made, but only for such as are cleansed in the precious blood of the Lamb. No place is found for them that believe not in Jesus; and if any love their sins better than God's salvation, the New Jerusalem is not for them. The lie of the devil, that was the primary cause of ruining the Adamic creation, will never enter there.

The perfection of His economy: "And he showed me a pure river of water of life, clear as crystal, proceeding out of the throne of God and the Lamb" (Rev. 22:1). A phenomenal river issues from the eternal throne with crystal clearness that never can be defiled, flowing with exhaustless blessings for the inhabitants of the city. "A heavenly river, belonging to a heavenly city, and for the use and joy of its heavenly people." The garden of Eden had its river for creation blessing (Gen. 2:10-14). Redemption's blessing has flowed for all as a river from the smitten Rock (Ex. 17:5-6). Spiritual blessings in a present age flow from our glorified Lord in heaven as "rivers of living water" through the Holy Spirit (Jn. 7:38-39). Millennial blessings in the kingdom will be as a mighty river issuing from the temple, ever deepening as it flows, flooding earth with God-given prosperity and peace (Ezek. 47:1-5). So the New Jerusalem will have its bountiful supply of living waters, unceasingly rolling from the living source, the exhaustless flow of the divine life "of God and the Lamb." With blessedness and joy we shall drink of the river of God with its pure, crystal waters of eternal life.

There is also a phenomenal tree, "the tree of life" (Rev. 22:2), to beautify the city and supply it with perennial fruit. Shall we eat? Why not! Glorified saints may eat, although under no necessity. Jesus ate in His resurrection body (Lk. 24:41-43). Angels ate of Sarah's cakes and of Abraham's tender calf (Gen. 18:6-8). Yet there is much more that is moral and spiritual connected with eating. (See Jn. 6:54-58; Mt. 26:26-28; Rev. 2:7.) In that realm of eternal economy, we shall drink Life water and eat Life fruit forever! Even the nations below will receive beneficial healing from the "leaves of the tree."

The perfection of His reign: And "the throne of God and of the Lamb shall be in it" (Rev. 22:3). The description of the city has been chiefly external until the throne comes into view in our chapter. Now John is brought right to the throne, the heart of all the city's glory, and the eternal occupants: "God and the Lamb." It is the throne of the eternal and absolute Ruler, One who once was slain, but lives to reign with His glorified saints unto the ages of ages. The universal administration will be shared by God, the Lamb, and His glorified saints also—for "His servants shall serve Him" as eternal joint-heirs by His grace (Rom. 8:17-18). From the external glories, we are at last brought to the most intimate and greatest revelation—to gaze at last on the face of the Lamb, possessed of inexpressible beauty and love. The centrality of all the glory is this: "They shall see His face" (Rev. 22:4), transfiguring us eternally into His own glorious likeness. "And His name shall be in their foreheads." The vision of His face will never be dimmed nor obscured, for the Spirit again writes, "And there shall be no night there" (compare Rev. 21:25). So the perfections of the Lamb shall be ours with everlasting joy and we shall "reign for ever and ever!"

> *"The Bride eyes not her garment,*
> *But her dear Bridegroom's face.*
> *I will not gaze at glory,*
> *But on my King of Grace.*
> *Not at the crown He giveth,*
> *But on His pierced hands.*
> *The Lamb is all the glory,*
> *Of Immanuel's Land!"*
>
> (Anne Ross Cousin)

24
Strong & Steadfast

"Cease ye from man, whose breath is in his nostrils: for wherein is he to be accounted of?" Thus said Isaiah as he described the coming age of the Lord and His judgments descending on this world (Isa. 2:22). Man's greatest strength is weakness at best. For the Lord "taketh not pleasure in the legs of a man" (Ps. 147:10). The legs of a man bend beneath their burdens and, writes Solomon graphically, "in the day when the keepers of the house shall tremble...the strong men shall bow themselves" (Eccl. 12:3). The Lord Jesus described the conditions of the world which will proceed His return, saying, "Upon the earth distress of nations, with perplexity; the sea and the waves roaring; men's hearts failing them for fear." (Read Lk. 21: 25-26.)

Today, in these circumstances we must rest in the strength and steadfastness of Christ alone. In contrast to weak men, the bride describes her beloved as one with "legs...as pillars of marble" in Song of Solomon 5:15. This figurative description symbolizes that both strength and steadfastness are the Lord's alone.

THE SYMBOL OF STRENGTH

Our redemption rests on those "pillars of marble," for on Him was laid the weight of His people's sin, from the beginning to the end of the world. (See Isa. 53:6.) Did He bear them all? Absolutely! For His legs are "pillars of marble." In eloquent expression of His unfailing strength, His legs were not broken on the cross (Jn. 19:31-36). The legs of the railer crucified with him were broken. The legs of the penitent thief were broken, for his own strength was weakness and all his help was in Another.

But they broke not the legs of the Lord Jesus, for His own Father, though bruising Him (Isa. 53:10), would grant a token of His loving care, to signify that everlasting strength is Christ's, even in the midst of weakness. No human or heavenly power dared to break those legs, for infallible Scripture had declared that "a bone of Him shall not be broken." He was the true Passover Lamb (Ex. 12:46; Num. 9:12; and 1 Cor. 5:7).

The maintaining of His Church is given to His care and His unfailing strength alone assures its safety and permanence. Can He sustain the weight? Listen to His words: "On this Rock I will build My assembly, and hades' gates shall not prevail against it" (Mt. 16:18, JND Trans.). No power can prevail to destroy His Church for His legs are "pillars of marble," possessing unfailing strength (read Eph. 5:25-27). The glorious consummation of His Bride is definitely assured.

The burdens of all His followers are cast upon Him. "Cast thy burden upon the Lord, and He shall sustain thee" (Ps. 55:22; 1 Pet. 5:7) All their fears and countless burdens He invites them to place on Himself. Thousands upon thousands have done it! Thousands are doing it! Child of God, are you doing it? Can He endure all the weight? Yes, for his legs are "pillars of marble."

THE SYMBOL OF STEADFASTNESS

Steadfastness is symbolized as well as strength. In all men, from Adam downward, "the unequal legs of the lame" have been seen; halting, stumbling, and falling in the way. But the legs of the "last Adam" (1 Cor. 15:45) are pillars of marble, upright, even, steadfast, and unmovable.

Satan proved them (read Mt. 4:1-11; Lk. 4:1-13). Jesus walks wearily from the wilderness, hungry, with knees weak through fasting. Satan tests whether those upright limbs will bend before him. "If Thou be the Son of God, command that these stones be made bread." Stoop! Eat and satisfy Thy hunger! says the devil. He stoops not, but walks on, saying, "Man shall not live by bread alone." He does not bend for His legs are pillars of marble.

Satan takes Him to a pinnacle of the temple, saying, "Cast

Thyself down..." Even on the narrow confines of the pinnacle, Jesus stands still and does not move. What a very dangerous place is a religious pinnacle! He answers Satan, "Thou shalt not tempt the Lord thy God." His legs are "pillars of marble."

Satan makes one more desperate effort, more daring; for nothing will satisfy him but the prostrate bending of those pillars in obeisance. The kingdoms of the world and their glory are shown the Lord. "All these will I give Thee, If Thou wilt fall down and worship me." But the temptation is vain. The pillars move not. He will never bend His knees to Satan. "Get thee hence Satan," is the reply and Satan flees, confounded and defeated. He must add his reluctant testimony to the Bride's: "His legs *are* pillars of marble!" Every man has bowed the knee to sin and Satan, but not the Son of God. What steadfastness!

The saints prove the steadfastness of His legs. For us His legs are still "pillars of marble" as He dwells at the right hand of God above. He is our great High Priest (Heb. 2:17-18; 4:14-16), the unfailing source of mercy and grace for our help in every time of need. He is our great Intercessor (Heb. 7:25; Rom. 8:34), steadfastly praying for His own in the present world. Read John 17 and digest His great High Priestly prayer. He is our great Advocate (1 Jn. 2:1-2), never failing to maintain our cause and our relationship with His Father above. Satan can often accuse of sin, for he is "the accuser of the brethren" (Rev. 12:10). But even in heaven Satan finds that our Advocate has "legs of pillars of marble."

The world will prove the steadfastness of His legs. He alone has the power and right to "set His right foot upon the sea, and the left foot on the earth" (Rev. 10:1-6). What a mighty description of His power is given, when He is about to take the kingdom of the world for Himself. What marvelous legs are these!

The world will know the power of those legs when "...His feet shall stand in that day upon the mount of Olives, which is before Jeruselam on the east, and the mount of Olives shall cleave in the midst thereof toward the east and toward the west a very great valley: and half of the mountain shall remove toward the north, and half of it toward the south" (read Zech. 14). At the glory of His return to the earth, Jesus will manifest

His great strength and steadfastness as He establishes His Millennial Kingdom. The world will find that His legs are "pillars of marble!" for "the Lord shall be King over all the earth" (Zech 14:9).

Our present encouragement is this: "If we believe not, yet He abideth faithful: He cannot deny Himself" (2 Tim. 2:13). Thank God for His strength and steadfastness! Annie Johnson Flint graphically compares the thread of our faith and the cable of His faithfulness:

> *Though waves and billows o'er me pass*
> *In whelming floods of ill,*
> *Within the haven of God's love*
> *My soul is anchored still:*
> *For though the stress and strain of life*
> *My thread of faith may break,*
> *The cable of His faithfulness*
> *No storm can ever shake.*

Beloved, let us always remember: "His legs are as pillars of marble" (Song of Sol. 5:15).

25
She Loved Much

One of the highest commendations given by the Lord was to a woman "which was a sinner" (Lk. 7:37). He declared of her, "she loved much" (Lk. 7:47). Why such great love? Let us consider her conversion in Luke 7:37-38. Seven facts about her are given, not what she said, but what she did. Actions do speak louder than words!

She came to His feet, the place of decision. She sought the Saviour only, being oblivious to all others present. Jesus was there, and to Him alone she came. What did others matter; she wanted Him. Like the prodigal of Luke 15, the language of her heart was, "I will arise and go to Him, saying, I have sinned against heaven and before Thee." It was the most momentous decision of her life, for time and eternity!

She stood at His feet, the place of submission. Silent, immovable, she stands in His presence. His words of mercy, love, and grace had won her heart, and now she indicates her yieldedness to His claims. It is as though she says, like Saul of Tarsus, "Lord, what wilt Thou have me to do?" (Acts 9:6). He had knocked at her heart's door and now she stood in the servant's place at His feet.

She wept at His feet, the place of true contrition. Her lips were inaudible, but with unmistakable proof of sorrow and remorse for her past—and blessed relief for the forgiveness she had found—her tears of love and joy flowed over His feet. It expressed the language of a sincere penitent as though to say, "Wash me thoroughly from mine iniquity, and cleanse me from my sin" (Ps. 51:2). "Out of much affliction and anguish of heart...with many tears" (2 Cor. 2:4), she poured on His feet her token of contrition—the best place and before the best Person to weep!

She washed His feet, the place of humiliation. Simon failed in hospitality to His illustrious Guest, but her tears flowed copiously upon His feet and washed them. She could stoop no lower than He Himself did, when washing the disciples' feet in the upper room (Jn. 13). Was she not fulfilling those words of exhortation written later by Paul: "Let this mind be in you which was also in Christ Jesus" (Phil. 2:5)? She now possessed the lowly mind of her Saviour. In humility, she washed His blessed feet.

She wiped His feet, the place of consecration. When the Lord washed His disciples' feet, He used basin and towel, but she took her glory—"but if a woman have long hair, it is a glory to her" (1 Cor. 11:15)—and thus she wiped His feet. The truth of Romans 12:1 was fulfilled, the yielding of her "body," presenting herself as "a living sacrifice, holy, acceptable unto God, which is your reasonable service." What an act of literal consecration!

She kissed His feet, the place of affection. Not once, but unceasingly, she planted her kisses on those blessed feet (Lk. 7:45). Judas planted a betrayal kiss on the blessed cheek of the Lord, but "this woman hath not ceased to kiss My feet," said Jesus. But why His feet? "How beautiful...are the feet of Him that bringeth good tidings" (Isa. 52:7). They were the most beautiful feet in all humanity to her—and should be to us.

She anointed His feet, the place of adoration. The precious, fragrant, anointing oil upon His feet was the climactic evidence of her appreciation and love. Like Mary of Bethany, the odor of the ointment must have filled the house. It was worship in the Spirit and rejoicing in Christ Jesus (Phil. 3:3).

Her attitude and actions demonstrated the completeness of her salvation without a word being spoken. Have we demonstrated it where it alone can be done to please Him? At His feet is the place where we too can "love much"!

Part Three
The Lord the Spirit

26
The River of God

"I will give them water," said the Lord concerning Israel in the desert. So today, God Himself is the solitary source of blessing for His people. In all our present journey through this world, a wilderness path, there is not one iota of earthly resource that can minister to the spiritual needs of the saints. This fact should be practically acknowledged by the people of God. None other but God alone is the infinite, unfailing, and perfect stream of blessing for His people on earth. Paul the Apostle truthfully testified that "our sufficiency is of God" and that means for all things.

Water is the symbol of God's blessing for His creatures on earth. How abundantly the types of Scriptures suggest this fact, first in God's creation blessing in the garden of Eden; for "a river went out of Eden to water the garden" (Gen. 2:10). Also in redemption blessing, symbolized in Exodus 17:5-6. From the smitten rock, "the waters gushed out, and the streams overflowed" (Ps. 78:15-20). Even the millennial earth and its blessing, is symbolized in Ezekiel 47:1-12 by the river that flows from the altar of the millennial temple, becoming "waters to swim in, a river that could not be passed through." Its counterpart is seen in Revelation 22:1, where the heavenly glory of that day is also typified by "a pure river of water of life, clear as crystal, proceeding out of the throne and of the Lamb."

Bringing this symbol into application for the saints today, the present ministry of the Holy Spirit of God is symbolized by the Lord Jesus as "rivers of living water." John 7:37-39 expresses His exact statement, saying, "In the last day, that great day of the feast, Jesus stood and cried, saying, If any man thirst, let him come unto Me and drink. He that believeth on Me, as the Scripture hath said, out of his belly shall flow rivers of living water. But this spake He of the Spirit, which they that believe on Him should receive."

Let us carefully remember, however, that the "rivers of living water" which the Spirit of God ministers from our risen Head in heaven to us below, flow only through the channel of the Word of God to our hearts. Water not only symbolizes blessing from God in the Scripture, but is often a type of the Word of God (see Jn. 3:5; Jn. 13:2-20; Eph. 5:26). Thus when God the Holy Spirit ministers the "spiritual blessings" that are ours in Christ (Eph. 1:3), never forget that the instrument used by the Spirit to cause the waters of blessing to flow, is the Word of God. So when His people are properly gathered together, the Spirit of God is the Divine Agent who unlocks the precious Word of God for His people. "We have received, not the spirit of the world, but the Spirit which is of God, that we might know the things that are freely given to us of God" (1 Cor. 2:12).

Did not God fulfill His divine promise to bless His people in the days of the Apostles? Some of us also know, that again in the Nineteenth Century many of the saints proved that God was still able to give His people "water." Many in that day sought the Holy Scriptures of truth for God's revealed mind and purposes concerning His Church on earth. They gathered together in scriptural companies, in obedience to His command, acknowledged New Testament truths in relation to Him, seeking by His grace to keep His Word and not deny His name (Rev. 3:8). Then what did God do? He kept His promise: "I will give them water"—and such a stream of spiritual ministry flowed to and through those saints that it has been unequalled since. Its flow is still being enjoyed by many of us today, but how sad is the fact that at large, "the rivers of living water" are not being experienced as then. Oh, that God's command may be heard and answered: His promise is unfailing and our obedience will result in His blessing, for has He not said, "I *will* give them water."

27
Another Comforter

In John 14 through 16, we have revealed by the Lord Jesus the complete and definite work of the Holy Spirit when He would be sent to earth. To His beloved disciples in the Upper Room, ere He went to the Cross, the Lord revealed the personal actions of the Spirit upon the earth during our present age.

1. *The Reality of His Person:* Let us be mindful always that the Spirit of God is definitely a Person, and that divine, equal with the Father and the Son. The Son testifies to this equality in John 14:16, saying, "And I will pray the Father, and He shall give you another Comforter." He, the Son, is a Comforter also and for His own; but the Spirit likewise is a Comforter. The word "comforter" implies One that is "called to one's side." As J. N. Darby aptly expresses this truth, "One who carries on the cause of anyone and helps him. This Christ did on earth; this He does now in heaven (1 Jn. 2:1) and the Spirit of God on earth manages our cause, our affairs for us."

2. *The Reality of His Abiding Presence:* "that He may abide with you forever" (v. 16). The blessed truth of the constant presence of the Holy Spirit with the Christian believer is taught here. The saints of the Old Testament were not so privileged, for David's prayer in Psalm 51:11 reveals His fear of losing the presence of God's Spirit. Well might he fear, for it had happened to King Saul (1 Sam. 28:15). How precious, then, is this promise of the Lord Jesus that the Holy Spirit will "abide with you forever." Let us enjoy and experience daily this blessed fact.

3. *The Reality of His Indwelling Presence:* Added to the above

truth is the most significant fact of Christianity, expressed at the end of verse 17 with these words: "For He dwelleth with you and shall be *in you*." No previous dispensation and no future dispensation has known or will know this truth of an indwelling Spirit in each believer. When we see the Son of God taking the form of our humanity as a babe in Bethlehem, we worship in adoration, hearing the prophet say, "They shall call His name Emmanuel, which being interpreted is, God *with us*" (Mt. 1:23). We gaze in tearful wonder and contrition of heart as we behold the same blessed One on the Cross of sin and shame for us. God "spared not His own Son, but delivered Him up for us all" (Rom. 8:32), and we echo the apostle's words; "If God be *for us,* who can be against us?" (Rom. 8:31). What should we say and do, as we contemplate the incomparable importance of the truth of Christianity? Christ has done His redemptive work: He is now glorified above and His promise has been fulfilled. The Holy Ghost has come and He indwells each believer. Surely the amazing significance of the present age is: God in us—the Holy Spirit dwelling within! Is it a living reality to us?

4. *Our personal knowledge of the Comforter:* In verse 17, the Lord Jesus said to His disciples, "Ye know Him." Does the world know the Spirit of God? No! for "the world cannot receive Him, because it seeth Him not; neither knoweth Him, but ye know Him." This knowing is *ginosko,* the form meaning objective knowledge, what a man has learned or acquired.

How wonderful the truth our Lord here implies concerning our personal knowledge of the Holy Spirit! We have acquired, by grace divine, a personal knowledge of the Comforter, the Holy Spirit of God. It is a twofold knowledge; as being with us and also being in us. This blessing belongs to every believer in the present dispensation of God's grace, but do we experimentally enjoy this knowledge? May God grant that we shall enter into these living truths in everyday experience, for Christ's sake.

114

28
The Temple of the Spirit

"What? know ye not that your body is the temple of the Holy Ghost which is in you, which ye have of God, and ye are not your own? For ye are bought with a price: therefore glorify God in your body, and in your spirit, which are God's (1 Corinthians 6:19-20).

Previous and future temples of God: There have been four divinely recognized buildings on earth acknowledged as God's temples: the tabernacle of Moses (1500-1000 BC); the temple of Solomon (1000-586 BC); the temple of Zerubbabel (515 BC-70 AD); and the temple of our Lord's body (Jn. 2:21). [*Editor's note:* Herod's Temple was simply the extension and beautification of Zerubbabel's Temple. Herod enlarged the temple platform by extending the retaining walls and building a kind of stone table over Mount Moriah. He also increased the height of the temple to approximately 100 feet, although he did not change the floor-plan. He added many out-buildings and the ill-fated gold crown around the top of the temple. It was this gold which ran between the stones when Titus sacked and burned the city in AD 70, causing the Romans to remove each stone from every other, thus fulfilling our Lord's prophecy. The Jews today still refer to Herod's Temple as the Second Temple.]

There are probably three temples in the future: the temple of the last days (Mt. 24:15; 2 Thess. 2:4, Rev. 11:1-2); the temple of the Millennium (Ezek. 40-44); and the temple of the New Jerusalem (Rev. 21:3, 22), existing in eternal glory.

The present temple of God: The Church on earth is divinely recognized as this: not the material edifices or organizations of Christendom, so-called, but the "living stones built up a spiritual house" (1 Pet. 2:5). The present testimony of God is seen in three ways: a universal aspect (Eph. 2:21), which embraces all believers; a local aspect (1 Cor. 3:16-17), which is the local gathering of believers, as in Corinth; an individual aspect, (1 Cor. 6:19-20), clearly presented as the physical body of the Christian.

The individual temple: One of the greatest truths of this dispensation of Christianity is this fact: "Your body is the temple of the Holy Ghost"! The body of each believer has become God's sanctuary, indwelt by the Spirit of God. A careful reading of Romans 8:9 and Ephesians 1:13 will show this distinguishing fact. How greatly God has honored us, yet with this He has also given great responsibility. Each believer can say, "I am God's temple!" God has built one shrine on earth during this age, as in the past and future of Judaism, but throughout the world He has distributed His "temples," living, walking, speaking, singing and working for Him and for His glory. They are His spiritual temples, commissioned to glorify Him in the present scene of evil. What kind of "temple" are you? What kind am I?

God's concern for His temples: A careful study of 1 Corinthians reveals to us a very unfortunate and disorderly condition existing among the saints. They were not "spiritual" but "carnal" Christians. The proof is seen in the few following facts: they neglected the ministry of God's Word, their only spiritual food for spiritual growth (1 Cor. 3:1-2); they showed the spirit of envy and strife toward each other, which promoted the existence of divisions among them (1 Cor. 3:3-4); they allowed to stay in their midst a brother who was guilty of a gross, moral sin (1 Cor. 5); others had filed lawsuits against their Christian brethren in the courts of the world, rather than suffering wrong or attempting to settle their troubles between each other in the spiritual way (1 Cor. 6); that holy feast of remembrance, the Lord's Supper, was being held in a very unworthy manner, bringing the judgment of God upon many believers (1 Cor. 11); in the public gatherings of saints, instead of godly order and edification being seen, their actions were producing confusion and discord, to their own dis-

116

grace and God's displeasure.

All these things gave evidence of conduct and character that was unbecoming to those who were the temples of God. For this reason Paul must write: "And I, brethren, could not speak unto you as unto spiritual, but as unto carnal, even as unto babes in Christ" (1 Cor. 3:1). God had thus a perfect right to be jealous of His people and seek their restoration to a spiritual condition. Likewise today, He is still jealous of our faithfulness and devotion, rightfully demanding spirituality from those whom He has redeemed through His beloved Son.

The cause of carnality: The probable source of carnality in a believer can be traced to the ignoring of the Spirit of God dwelling in the body. "Do ye not know that your body is the temple of the Holy Spirit which is in you, which ye have of God; and ye are not your own? For ye are bought of a price; glorify now then God in your body" (1 Cor. 6:19-20, JND Trans.). This fact was being ignored or forgotten by the believers in Corinth. Has it not been the unfortunate evil in the Church from the days of Ananias and Sapphira? (see Acts 5). Their unbelief in the immediate presence of the Holy Ghost led them to obey the voice of Satan rather than God. If they had shown their faith in His presence, never would they have committed their terrible sin! Yet we also can stand condemned as having ignored the Person of the Holy Spirit in our own hearts and lives.

The responsibility of a believer: There are three facts to realize from the Scripture portion in 1 Corinthians 6:19-20: 1. The Owner of the temple is the Holy Spirit of God. We are not our own: we belong to Another. "Under new management" should be placed across the life by every Christian now rejoicing in salvation. 2. The price paid for the "temple" is beyond all human computation—"Ye are bought with a price." The tabernacle of Moses and the temple of Solomon were erected at fabulous costs! But, "ye were not redeemed with corruptible things as silver and gold...but with the precious blood of Christ, as of a lamb without blemish and without spot" (1 Pet. 1:18-19). A quiet, sober meditation on the infinite sacrifice of Christ on the Cross will prove to you and me something of the great price paid for us. 3. The purpose of the temple is: "Glorify now then

God in your body." In the creation of man, it was God's objective that he should glorify his Creator, but that was made completely impossible through the entrance of sin. Now, however, through grace God can take the body of His child and use it for His glory. This is the purpose of the Spirit of God's indwelling in these "temples" of clay.

With such divine claims, we recognize why God should say to us, each one: "I beseech you, therefore, brethren, by the compassions of God, to present your bodies a living sacrifice, holy, acceptable unto God, which is your intelligent service. And be not conformed to this world, but be transformed by the renewing of your mind, that ye may prove what is the good and acceptable and perfect will of God" (Rom. 12:1-2, JND Trans.). How simple, yet how sublime, is our responsibility. It is not to seek more of the Holy Spirit, but rather to allow the Spirit of God to use His property, by yieldedness and surrender of the "temple" to Him! Moment by moment, hour by hour, day by day, and year by year, till death or the coming of the Lord terminates our earthly existence, this should be our obedient act.

May God use these meditations to stir the soul exercise of all who are His people, that we shall seek faithfully to be "temples" for His glory in every way, for the honor of our Lord Jesus Christ.

29
Resources for Difficult Days

"This know, that in the last days perilous times shall come" (2 Tim. 3:1), prophesied the apostle Paul, giving a detailed description of the moral and spiritual dangers in the verses following (vv. 2-5). There is no promise of spiritual recovery to pristine beauty and strength; only further emphasis of increasing apostasy and declension as "evil men...wax worse and worse, deceiving and being deceived" (2 Tim. 3:12). In such perilous days, we need a prayerful and thoughtful appraisal of our spiritual resources, coupled with a determination to appropriate them for our blessing and for God's glory. God has always provided the necessary resources for His children in every age, but we must know what they are and how to use them. Let us consider briefly three important, available resources provided today.

THE HOLY SPIRIT

The Spirit of God is a real, living Person, one of the members of the Godhead; and though He has not taken human form as did the Son of God, yet the reality of His personal being is definitely taught in Scripture. He bears a distinct and special relationship to the children of God today which was not known in past ages and not to be known in future dispensations. Listen to the words of our Lord from John 14:16, promising the Spirit of God to His disciples, when our Saviour was about to depart back to heaven: "I will pray the Father, and He shall give you another Comforter, that He may abide with you forever."

Consider first, the greatness of His Person: "Another Comforter." The words imply "Another of the same kind, like Myself"—One who is equal in His Person to Christ our Lord. The word "Comforter" also conveys the following meaning: One who carries on the cause of anyone and helps him. This the Saviour did for His own when on earth; this He now does for them in heaven (1 Jn. 2:1-2), but the Holy Spirit has been given to manage our cause, our affairs on earth for us now. He has been given to be our Helper—to control, direct, and take charge of us; in all our daily pathway to manage us and all things on our behalf. Do we permit Him to? What is our attitude toward His Person? Do we yield ourselves to His government? Great is our responsibility and, when obeyed, greater still will be the proof of His strength in us and through us.

Consider also the irrevocable character of the Spirit of God's presence: "That He may abide with you forever." We may vex, grieve, or quench the Holy Spirit, but no conduct of ours will ever send Him away. Blessed grace of our God! Should we not value the presence of this Holy One with us and in us? Should we not make complete surrender to His sovereign presence and power by yielding our beings to His control? He is our resource of strength today and will be to the end of our days!

THE WORD OF GOD

God's Word is one of the greatest sources of strength for us also, an unfailing channel of divine help for those who diligently seek its truths. Timothy was admonished, "But continue thou in the things which thou hast learned and hast been assured of" (in 2 Tim. 3:14). We must maintain our affection and appreciation for God's Word. It is the source of vital strength for us and has a dual effect in us according to the context of 2 Timothy 3:15-17.

First, "the Holy Scriptures...are able to make thee wise unto salvation through faith which is in Christ Jesus." We correctly state that God's Word is to bring us into the knowledge of salvation, yet Timothy was in the midst of spiritual dangers from which he needed deliverence, as we are surrounded by spiritual difficulties today. The Word of God imparts guidance for us, to save us from and out of the dangers that would overcome us in "the last days." Do we daily use the Book to this end?

Second, for our spiritual growth and maturity, completing our spiritual equipment, through doctrine, reproof, correction, and instruction, the Word of God will prove all-sufficient to increase our usefulness for His glory in "the last days." What is my attitude towards God's Word? Do I use it and daily seek its divine strength and comfort for my soul? Let me say with the Psalmist, "How sweet are Thy words unto my taste! Yea, sweeter than honey to my mouth" (Ps. 119:103).

THE THRONE OF GRACE

Weaknesses and infirmities harrass us; but God has provided access to a throne in heaven, from which the Lord Jesus Christ is able to minister the needed help for us on earth. Listen to the Amplified Version describe the throne of grace: "The throne of God's unmerited favor; that we may receive mercy and find grace to help in good time for every need—appropriate help and well-timed help, coming just when we need it."

A living, loving, risen, and glorified Lord, as our Great High Priest, is upon that throne above on our behalf. Through the sufferings on earth He endured, as our merciful and great High Priest in things related to God...He is able to run to the cry of those who are being tempted and tested and tried (Heb. 2:17-18). What a blessed source of strength this is for you and me! Do I use it? Am I constantly taking advantage of every opportunity in my testings, to prove the merits of the Lord's grace from above just when I need it? The Throne of Grace is another great provision for my spiritual strength in "difficult days."

Past emergencies of spiritual peril, as recorded in the Word, indicate that God's servants who manifested spiritual strength in apostate and unholy days, were men who used their knees. Glance with me at Elijah on Mount Carmel during Israel's apostasy. While "Ahab went up to eat and to drink...Elijah went up to the top of Carmel; and he cast himself down upon the earth, and put his face between his knees" (1 Ki. 18:42). Look into the chambers of Ezra the scribe, in the days of the peoples' transgression. With heaviness of heart, he cries, "I fell upon my knees, and spread out my hands unto the Lord my God." Travel in memory into godless and heathen Babylon, to witness the consistent behavior of Daniel: "He went into his house, and his windows being open in his chambers toward Jerusalem, he kneeled upon his knees three times a day, and prayed, and gave thanks before his God, as he did aforetime" (Dan. 6:10). The beloved Paul reveals his love and concern for the saints at Ephesus, saying, "For this cause I bow my knees unto the Father of our Lord Jesus Christ..." (Eph. 3:14). The dying Stephen ends his powerful testimony on his knees, as he "kneeled down, and cried with a loud voice, Lord, lay not this sin to their charge" (Acts 7:60).

Well has Isaiah written long ago, "But they that wait upon the Lord shall renew their strength; they shall mount up with wings as eagles; they shall run, and not be weary; and they shall walk, and not faint" (Isa. 40:31). Here is a source of spiritual and divine strength when properly used. Let us obey the exhortation of the Psalmist, "O come, let us worship and bow down: let us kneel before the Lord our maker" (Ps. 95:6).

Other truths concerning our resources could readily be given; but here are three sources of strength we should be availing ourselves of daily. The Spirit of God waits to be used; likewise the Word of God expects the believer to appropriate its precious strength; the lovely, risen and glorious Lord above exceedingly longs for us to wait before Him at the Throne of Grace in order to obtain from such sources of divine strength all we have need of to stand "in the last days." May the Holy Spirit help us to prove our God is able to keep and to use His own today.

Scripture Index